HOLIDAY WALKS
in

Graham Beech

Published by: Sigma Leisure – an imprint of
Sigma Press, Stobart House, Pontyclerc, Penybanc Road
Ammanford, Carmarthenshire SA18 3HP, UK

British Library Cataloguing in Publication Data
A CIP record for this book is available from the British Library.

ISBN: 978-1-85058-856-6

Printed by: Akcent Media Ltd

Cover Photographs:
Top: Lighthouse looking over Port de Sóller
Middle left: The Island of Dragonera
Middle right: Bay of Port de Sóller
Bottom left: Puig de Santa Eugenia
Bottom right: Poppies at Banyalbufar

Photographs within the book: the author, except where stated

Maps: Michael Gilbert and Bute Cartographics

Thanks to . . .

Diana – for accompanying me on many of the walks, encouraging me to write the book, and for not worrying *too* much when I broke all the rules and walked alone in the mountains.

Brian – fri~~end, walking companion, proofreader and~~ provider of invaluable ~~...~~

Disclaim~~er~~

Whilst ever~~...~~ this book, no
warranty is ~~...~~ accuracy or
completene~~...~~ Neither the
Author nor ~~...~~ amage arising
by virtue of ~~...~~ ce contained
within this ~~...~~d. Except as
specifically ~~...~~s in this book
do not nec~~...~~

Contents

Introducing Mallorca

After walkers have explored their local patch, thoughts may turn to overseas destinations – where the days are longer, the weather kinder and the scenery certainly more unusual. Mallorca – once thought of as just a sun and sand destination – might not be the first place to consider, but it really ought to be high on your list. You can be there in a couple of hours or so and, with a not-too-early flight, enjoy an afternoon walk on your day of arrival! Accommodation is excellent value, visitors are made very welcome, and there are walking routes for every taste – from leisurely coastal strolls to serious mountain hikes. And you don't need to go walking in an organised group – all you need is a plane ticket, somewhere to stay and this book!

You can, of course, just choose the walks that appeal to you and start walking. However, this short introduction will add to your enjoyment, and help you to appreciate the heritage of the island.

Location & Geography

Mallorca is one of the Balearic islands and, according to the *Encyclopaedia Britannica*, its old Latin name was 'Balearis Major' – the larger Balearic island. The islands were also known to the Greeks and, indeed, the *Balearis* part may be derived from the Greek 'ballein', meaning 'to throw' (hence, also, 'ballistics') as the early inhabitants were renowned – and feared – for their expertise with a slingshot.

The island lies off the eastern coast of Spain and is almost equidistant from France and North Africa, which have both been important export destinations for agricultural products. It measures 76km north-south and 96km east-west, with a surface area of 3,650 square kilometres – over 70% of the total area of the Balearics – and a coastline of almost 550km. There are three main bays – those of Palma, Alcúdia and Pollença – but the real gems are the countless smaller inlets and coves that are scattered all around the coast, some of which are visited on the walks in this book.

The varied geography of Mallorca offers a wide range of walking opportunities. The central plain – 'Es Pla' – is a gently rolling landscape of extensive farmland and picturesque villages. The north-west has the dramatic Serra de Tramuntana limestone mountain range, about 100km long and up to 12km wide: that's about half the total area of Snowdonia or the Lake District, but with more mountains per square kilometre. The mountains extend from Cap de Formentor in the north, all the way to Sant Elm and Dragonera in the south-west. The highest is Puig Mayor (1450m), surmounted by a military communications complex, and not generally open to the public. Other peaks include Massanella (1340m), L'Ofre (1080m), Teix (1060m) and Galatzó (1025m). The south-east has a parallel upland area, the Sierra de Llevant, with peaks up to about 500m; this region is famous for its limestone caves and subterranean lakes.

Despite the low rainfall, much of the island is surprisingly green, thanks to the subterranean aquifers from which water is pumped. Windmills were traditionally used for this purpose – there used to be almost 1000 of them on the Balearics, and many hundreds on Mallorca, but most are electrical nowadays. They are now regarded as minor national monuments and there is a web site, www.mallorcawindmills.com, with locations, designs and photographs.

History

Mallorca is rich in history and some walks in this book take you to sites built by the many races that have settled here. Ancient remains and cave drawings have been found throughout Mallorca dating from around 7000BC, when the population consisted of tiny communities scattered around the coast. Around 3000BC, domesticated livestock and arable crops became more important. From 2000BC, modest-sized Bronze Age settlements marked the appearance of greater social organisation. Around 1300BC, 'talayots' began to be constructed throughout the Balearics from large blocks of stone. Characteristic designs were adopted on each island: on Mallorca, talayots in the centres of villages were circular, with passages and small rooms; they may have had a religious function, though they were often in visual sight of each other, so may also have been used to warn of likely attacks. More functional buildings elsewhere in villages may have been used for accommodation. Over 400 talayotic sites have been found on Mallorca – for further information, visit www.spanisharts.com/arquitectura/imagenes/prehistoria/i_talayots.html

Throughout the island's turbulent history, Mallorca's favourable climate and fertile soil have attracted settlers. It also lies on the main trade routes of the Mediterranean, making for a useful stopping-off point during long voyages and, just as important, a convenient base for piracy. Tiring of attacks on their ships, the Romans, led by Quintus Cecilius Metellus, invaded in 123BC. They colonised the island, the main settlements being around present-day Palma and Alcúdia. Remains can still be seen, including the ruins of Pollentia (just outside Alcúdia) and the Puente Romana (Roman bridge) in Pollença. Also, the Palma to Alcúdia road closely follows the original Roman highway. During the Roman occupation, Christianity became the established religion, and Mallorca's first churches were built.

After the collapse of the Roman empire, the aptly named Vandals conducted a series of raids, finally occupying the island in AD465, destroying many of the churches and persecuting the Christian population. In AD534 Byzantine forces expelled the Vandals, Christianity was restored and Mallorca entered a more prosperous period, though this was short-lived because of the difficulty of running an outpost so far from Constantinople. The Arabic Moors from North Africa seized on this and a series of invasions progressively weakened the Byzantine occupiers. In AD902, the island became an annex of Córdoba, a city still famous for its magnificent mosque – one of the few not destroyed later by over-zealous Christians. The Moors brought new standards of civilisation and built terraces and irrigation systems for the cultivation of oranges, olives, and other traditional crops. They added a sophistication to the island's architecture and cuisine that is still evident today, together with many Arabic words that are components of place names throughout the island. Examples include many names that begin with "Al" such as Alcudia ("the hill"), Alfabia ("the reserve") and Algaida (the wood) and many less obvious ones including Biniaraix ("bini" for "houses of"), Bunyola (from "bujola" for "small vineyard") and Banyalbufar (from Banyalbahar, "built by the sea").

This happy state of affairs ended in the 11th and 12th centuries, with the Moors as the target of the Christian Crusades. After some unsuccessful attempts, King Jaime I of Aragon ("The Conqueror") landed at Santa Ponça in 1229 with a Catalan army of 15,000, which was confronted by 18,000 islanders. Battles ensued and Palma (then known by its Moorish name of Medina Mayurka) was under siege for almost three months before it fell to Jaime, who promptly divided the island amongst his chums and expelled the Moors.

After the death of Jaime I in 1276, Mallorca became an independent kingdom under Jaime II, the son of Jaime I. A renewed period of prosperity and culture ensued, during which many of the finest buildings were constructed. Peace, however, was fragile and control of the island passed between Catalonia and Aragon until 1349 when Jaime III was decisively defeated at the battle of Llucmajor and the Balearics again became part of Aragon. After almost 150 years of battles and scheming, Spain became a united country in 1492 under Ferdinand (of Aragon) and Isabella (of Castile) – the famed Catholic Monarchs. The next 150 years saw a period of expansionism for Spain, with the Conquistadors pillaging South America and returning with great riches. Mallorca, however, was neglected and became the target of pirates from Turkey and elsewhere.

In 1714, after the War of the Spanish Succession (1702-1713), Mallorca became a province of Spain and a long period of stability began. A steamship service between Mallorca and mainland Spain was inaugurated in 1837 and there was a considerable increase in the export of wine, almonds and other produce. The party came to an abrupt halt at the end of the 19th century when the island's grapevines were destroyed by *phylloxera* – aphid-like parasites that feed on the roots of the vines. This coincided with the closure of many shipyards, following the loss of most of Spain's former colonies. Unsurprisingly, many islanders emigrated to America and the Spanish mainland in search of better times.

Those who chose America did the smart thing, as the Spanish Civil War began in 1935 and lasted for four years. Although Mallorca escaped the worst excesses of this awful period, it suffered under Franco in much the same way as the rest of Spain. The Mallorquin language (a dialect of Catalan) was banned and the island's economy stagnated – until Mallorca became a tourist hot spot.

There had been a trickle of tourism in the 1920s, when Mallorca was visited mainly by the rich and famous, but the island only began to attract visitors in any number after the Second World War. Mass tourism began in the 1950s and accelerated rapidly after the death of Franco in 1975, when Spain and its islands were restored to democratic rule under the popular King Juan Carlos. In 1979, the Balearics became an autonomous region, and were again able to control their own destiny. The growth of high-rise hotel building has been curbed, and Mallorca is rapidly gaining a reputation for high-quality tourism and, of course, walking and cycling.

Transport

Getting there

There are flights from almost every European airport to Palma de Mallorca – try Skyscanner (www.skyscanner.net) or Flightline (www.flightline.co.uk) for the cheapest deals. Remember that if you buy a 'flight only' ticket in the UK you will not be compensated by ABTA in the event of airline failure and probably not covered by your holiday insurance policy; you should consider paying by credit (not debit) card as this will give some measure of financial compensation.

Public transport

Regular bus services connect all Mallorcan towns, but be sure to get current information from your hotel, Tourist Information Centres or the timetables at bus stops. Have your fare ready in advance or risk a grumpy bus driver. If you are planning your own walks, never rely on catching a bus from the end of your walk back to your start point – always use the public transport element at the beginning in case the walk takes longer than expected or the last bus of the day is cancelled!

There are trains between Palma and Inca, and between Palma and Sóller. There is also a fabulous old tram service between the town of Sóller and its port. Boats ply between the main harbours, for example those of Sóller and Cala Deià.

For greater flexibility, taxis will take you anywhere on the island. If you are travelling more than a mile or so, ask what the fare will be before committing yourself.

Car hire

Off the main bus routes, the easiest way to get to the start of a walk is with a hire car. Major car rental companies, plus several reputable Mallorcan ones, are based at Palma airport and at most resorts. If you are hiring from a company that you have not heard of, be sure to check the terms of the rental contract and examine the car carefully for scratches, dents and tyre condition before driving it away. Note that all drivers have to be listed on the hire document and you must keep this and your driving licence available for inspection by the police. **Hot tip:** your car hire agreement will include basic Collision Damage

Waiver and Theft clauses, but you may still be liable for a substantial part of the repair or replacement costs. To cover this 'excess', many hire companies offer additional insurance at ludicrously expensive daily rates; you can reduce this very, very substantially by taking out excess insurance before departure – just type "car hire excess" into Google for a pleasant surprise.

Accommodation

Many people stay in a hotel or apartment as part of a package. However, it is quite easy to plan your own itinerary, buy cheap flight tickets and book your own hotels, which are invariably better value than in the UK. There are many hotel booking sites including www.hotels.com and the Mallorca-based www.prima-travel.com, though you may get better rooms (and better rates in some cases) by contacting the hotel directly. For reports from previous visitors to your intended resort or hotel, visit the excellent Trip Advisor site at www.tripadvisor.com.

You can just turn up at the hotel of your choice and take a chance – but this can be frustrating in peak season. **Note:** from October to Easter, much of the north of the island closes down so far as accommodation is concerned. Also, inland Mallorca is very popular in springtime (April/May) when there is a mass invasion of cyclists, in addition to large groups of walkers, so the few hotels that are open in central and northern areas may be very busy.

For a touch of luxury at reasonable prices, an alternative to tourist hotels is the Agroturismo – a term used to describe farmhouses and other rural properties that have been converted to high-quality accommodation. Take a look at www.baleares.com/fincas/fincasing.htm or the interactive website www.agroturismo-balear.com operated by the Associació Agroturisme Balear.

The Binicomprat 'agroturismo' in Algaida

At the other end of the scale, there is more basic accommodation for walkers. This includes the sanctuaries and hermitages at Lluc, Petra, Randa and Pollença and the excellent mountain refuges of Tossals Verds, Muleta, Deià, Son Amer and Sa Trapa. A free leaflet is available from information centres and there is a very useful website, www.conselldemallorca.net/mediambient/pedra/ which describes the 150km Drystone Wall Route (Ruta de Pedra en Sec) linking the refuges of the Sierra de Tramuntana. Follow the links to 'refuges' and 'walking' for more information and for on-line booking.

Food & drink

These are much the same as the rest of southern Europe, but with local specialities such as ensaimadas (curly soft breakfast pastries), coca de verduras (delicious cheeseless pizza) and coca de trampo (similar but with added tuna), tumbet (a variation on ratatouille) or pa amb oli (bread with olive oil and, for example, tomatoes). Beer is standard Spanish, but do try the regional wines: both red and white wines from Binissalem's Jose Ferrer are excellent and there are many other producers, including Ribas, Miquel Oliver, Son Bordils, Binicomprat and the Banyalbufar cooperative. There are numerous websites but a good place to start is:

www.foodandwine.com/articles/mallorca-is-for-wine-lovers

Language

German, English and, particularly in the north, French are widely spoken but, off the beaten track, be prepared to speak a little Spanish. It will help you to understand a menu in a village restaurant – or to find your way if you get lost. If you only know a few words, just ask simple questions that will get simple answers. For example: "¿Dónde está el supermercado? – "Where is the supermarket?" – might result in complicated directions. But ask if it is near: "¿Hay un supermercado cerca de aquí?" – or to the right: "¿A la derecha?" – or the left: "¿A la izquierda?" and you will get agreement or disagreement. There's no space here for a comprehensive list of Spanish phrases, but there are dozens of excellent books and CDs. A couple of recommended publications are: Spanish Phrase Book (Berlitz). And you can always enrol on a "Holiday Spanish" course at home or even in Mallorca.

Quick Catalan

The traditional language of Mallorca is Mallorquin, a dialect of Catalan. Mallorquin was banned during the Franco period, so everybody can speak Castillian (standard) Spanish – but Mallorquin is being very actively promoted and is now used in much the same way that Welsh is spoken, alongside English, in Wales. Catalan is fairly similar to Spanish, but many words are different while some, such as adéu or pont, have more in common with French. Learning Spanish will be more than enough for most people so, rather than flicking through a second phrasebook, here are a few Catalan words and phrases that you can look for and maybe try out on your walks:

Greetings and courtesies:

Adéu	good-bye
Bon dia	good morning
Bona tarda	good afternoon
Bona nit	good night
Gràcies	thank you
Perdona	sorry
Salut	cheers
Si/no	yes/no
Si us plau	please

Additionally, you may see these words on signs or maps:

Avinguda	avenue
Ajuntament	Town Hall
Barranc	ravine or gorge
Ca'n ...	property of ... (sometimes "C'an" or just "Can")
Camin	footpath
Carrer	street
Coll	mountain pass
Coma	floor of valley
Correus	post office
Dreta	right
Ermita	hermitage/monastery
Esquerra	left
Font	spring
Llac	lake
Moli	mill
Mirador	viewpoint
Muntanya	mountain
Nou/noves	new
Penya	cliff
Pla	plain
Plaça	town/city square
Platja	beach
Pobla	village
Pont	bridge
Pou	well
Puig	mountain peak
Pujol	hill
Riu	river
Serra	mountain ridge
Sitja	circular area for the production of charcoal by the controlled burning of wood e.g. Holm Oak
Son ...	estate of ...
Talaia	lookout tower, usually on inland hill
Torre	coastal lookout tower or part of a castle etc.
Torrent	stream or river bed (dry except in flood conditions)
Vall	valley
Vell/velles	old

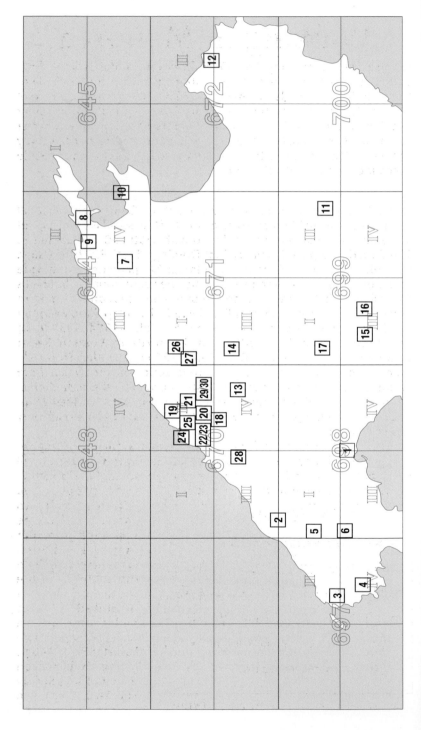

Walking in Mallorca

When is best? Almost any time! Overall, annual rainfall is light – from 1400mm in the mountains to just 300mm on the southern plain. Contrast that with England where the Lake District has an average of up to 3500mm. The best times for walking are September to October and February to May. Having said that, I have enjoyed better weather in January than in late March and, even in high summer you can enjoy some excellent walking in the mountains – so long as you take sensible precautions and plenty of water.

Maps

The 1:25,000 scale maps from the Instituto Geográfica Nacional (IGN) are a reasonable compromise. Most of the island is covered, but sometimes you may have to make do with 1:50,000 military maps. The Casa del Mapa in Palma (c/ Sant Domingo 11, C.P. 07001 Palma (Tel: (971) 22 59 45. E-mail: casadelmapa@a-palma.es) has a wide selection and a few other bookshops may be useful sources, but Sod's Law dictates that you won't find the ones you need, and it is best to buy before you arrive. UK suppliers include The Map Shop in Upton on Severn (web: www.themapshop.co.uk / tel: 01684 593146 or Freephone, 0800 085 4080) and Stanfords in London (web: www.stanfords.co.uk / tel: 020 7836 1321). For the Sierra de Tramuntana region, the highly regarded series of three maps from Editorial Alpina at a scale of 1:25,000, is probably the best choice. There is the 'Mallorca North and Mountains Tour & Trail Map' (Discovery Walking Guides. ISBN: 978-1-904946-33-5) though only at a scale of 1:40,000.

The problem with "official" maps is that while they may be topographically accurate, they are not designed for walkers – not all paths are shown and those that *are* shown may not be passable. However, by comparing them with the sketch maps in this book, you will be able to complete all of the walks and plan your own. The sketch maps are simplified indications of the route and are not intended as replacements for the real thing. The **location map**, facing, is based on the chart supplied by The Map Shop, with

KEY TO MAPS

— ❯ — Route and direction of Walk

- - - - - : Track   ═══ Road   △• Peak

Built-up area   ☐ Building   ⏆ Mast

♣ 🌳 Trees   ✳ Veiwpoint   ▮ Tower

🛆 Lighthouse   ⌘ Church, hermitage etc.

① Cross reference to text

Left, locations of walks; above, symbols used on maps

IGN map sheet reference numbers. Symbols used on the sketch maps are shown on page 9. For consistency, I have used place-names as shown on the IGN maps, so that readers are not confused by variations in spellings.

Access

Walking in Mallorca is not like England – there are very few guaranteed rights of access. Everywhere you walk, you will see "Coto Privado" supplemented by black and white signs. These simply indicate that the land is reserved for private hunting and they do not apply to walkers. Another popular sign, 'Camino Privado' usually only applies to vehicles. You are, in theory, allowed access to the coast and to sites of religious pilgrimage (many of these are on mountains) – but not necessarily by a circular route. There are a small number of national park areas (including the Victoria Park on the Alcúdia peninsula and the areas around Teix and Galatzó) but elsewhere access can be subject to the whim of the landowner and the determination, or otherwise, of the local authority. All of the routes in this book are believed to be "stable" and, with very few exceptions, have enjoyed unrestricted access for many years. I have tried to avoid areas that may lead to confrontation or where access is restricted to certain days of the week, or where payment is required. For example, access to Puig Roig is restricted and, for the privilege of climbing Massanella, there is a charge of €4. Some traditional coastal routes are also under threat: the once-popular walk to Castell del Rei, north of Pollença, is closed (though it may be re-opened to limited numbers) and, back in August 2000, Claudia Schiffer was reported to have blocked a path leading to one of the many 16th-century lookout towers. Worst of all, the island's much-touted GR221 long-distance trail has been blocked in Banyalbufar after a landowner presented his case in Palma and the court found in his favour!

Somewhat belatedly, the Island Council of Mallorca is promoting walking as a tourism activity. I wish the Council well, as it will be fighting investors hell-bent on coastal development for the super-rich. On the positive side, there is much more waymarking of the more popular paths and, longer-term, ecological groups are involved in the development of long-distance routes. However, there is a need for a greater commitment on the part of the local authorities and a determination to protect rights to traditional walking routes if Mallorca is to build a strong reputation with walkers.

If you are challenged by a landowner, please be courteous. Since many routes are permissive, antagonising local people may only worsen the situation. But, if you think that a route is blocked illegally, be sure to complain to the nearest town hall or tourist information office. Plenty of complaints may nip future problems in the bud!

Safety

Exercise the same care as when walking at home. If you can arrange it, walk with a small group in case of accidents so that somebody can stay with the injured party whilst others go for help. If you are a solo walker, make sure that somebody knows your route and expected return time. There is a mountain rescue service, which I have not yet used, but when walking alone be sure to leave details of your itinerary with a friend, relative or fellow guest rather than with the hotel receptionist. If possible, you should carry a mobile phone – if only to tell someone if you expect to return later than planned. In case of a *real* emergency, phone 112 or 062 – the former connects to the fire service (Bombers del Consell de Mallorca), the latter with the rural police (Guardia Civil).

Equipment

Wear suitable footwear: except for town trails and the easiest of strolls, boots are recommended as these will support your ankles and help to reduce the chances of slipping. Carry a small first-aid kit and go kitted out for all possibilities of weather. Island weather can change very quickly: I have experienced blue skies, clouds, showers and monsoon-style storms in Mallorca within just a couple of hours! On the mountains, cloud can drop quickly and thick mist can come rolling in from the sea quite unexpectedly. Remember also that strong sunlight can be a real problem, to the extent of ruining your holiday. You need sunglasses, a hat and sensible levels of protection to prevent sunburn. Take plenty of water – two litres for a day walk as a *minimum* in the summer.

It is essential to carry a map and compass, and possibly a GPS too – do not rely on the sketch maps in any guidebook for the simple reason that if you become disoriented, it is very easy to walk off the edge of the sketch map and into uncharted territory.

Distances and times

Distances have been measured from maps and adjusted to allow for ups and downs. An average speed of about 3km/hr is assumed, plus an allowance for climbs. Times quoted should be regarded as minima – so beware of starting late in the day.

Grades

In the information panel at the beginning of each walk, I have included a grading. **Easy** means a stroll on fairly level ground. **Moderate** involves some hills, but still within the capabilities of casual walkers. **Strenuous** describes a more serious mountain excursion for which you need to be reasonably fit.

Scenics

Amaze your friends with pictures of the high mountain ranges, the lush central plain, or breathtaking coastal scenery – Mallorca is a paradise for photographers as well as walkers! Come to Mallorca in the spring and see the wonderful display of flowers, including rockroses, orchids and freesias. Come at any time and admire the range of trees, many of which are still important commercially: olive trees, some from Biblical times, are everywhere – green olives are harvested from September to October and the black ones in November. Both are pickled in brine like any other pickle – try eating one straight from the tree to see why. The island is famous for its almond trees – in early spring, their blossom looks like a sprinkling of snow. Oranges and lemons grow abundantly in the fertile northern valleys, together with carobs, the fruits of which dangle like broad beans and are used for animal fodder, as the base for Palo (a liqueur with an acquired taste) and as a chocolate substitute. On second thoughts, there's no substitute for chocolate. Cherries, peaches, apricots, peaches and figs are also grown commercially. The Holm Oak (*Quercus ilex* – Holly Oak) is an evergreen relative of the English Oak. This was important for charcoal production and you can still see huge plantations of these trees on many of the walks in this book.

Mallorca on the Web

In addition to the specific sites already mentioned, there are literally thousands of websites relating to Mallorca, so finding useful ones is not easy. A good, general place to start is www.tourspain.co.uk, the web site for the Spanish Tourist Office, which includes an online brochure request service for popular destinations. The www.seemallorca.com site has lots of practical information on Mallorca and a nice slide show to get you in the mood for your trip. Good general sites for most of the towns and larger villages are www.a2zmallorca.com and www.mca-hotels.com/holidays-guide-mallorca. For news and current events, visit www.majorcadailybulletin.es, www.mallorcaweb.com/eng or www.newsmallorca.com/en/about.htm – the latter styling itself (quite reasonably) as the 'Independent Mallorca Tourist Board'.

Recommended reading

Insight Guide: Mallorca and Ibiza. ISBN: 978-9812340856

Landscapes of Mallorca, Valerie Crespi-Green (Sunflower Books, ISBN: 978-1856912044)

The Rough Guide to Mallorca and Menorca, ISBN: 978-1843537960

Walking in Mallorca, June Parker (Cicerone, ISBN: 978-1852844882)

Dragonera from above Sa Trapa (Walk 3)

Palma & The West

1. Palma
A walking tour of the city centre

Grade: easy

Distance: 8km

Time: 3 to 4 hours

Start & Finish: Plaça d'Espanya

How to get there: not recommended by car unless you can cope with city traffic, in which case underground car parks are clearly signposted. If arriving from the north, drive part-way then use the Metro: park your car (the Son Sardina station is clearly signed from the C711 main road) and enjoy a stress-free journey to the Plaça d'Espanya. Alternatively, there are buses from all over the island, also arriving at the Plaça d'Espanya.

Checklist: comfortable shoes, camera, money and plenty of stamina

Map: pick up a free street map from any of the information centres

Notes: plan your walk around the opening times of any places that you intend to visit. Sunday morning is a good choice as the centre is almost free of traffic and shoppers.

There is much more to Palma than its shops. The name is derived from the Roman city of Palmaria, known to the Moors as Medina Mayurka. Its maritime origins stretch back to the 13th century and its importance as a port continues to the present day. On this walking tour, you will see many reminders of maritime Palma, plus ancient churches, remains of Moorish occupation and the houses of wealthy merchants. You can easily spend a whole day on this tour alone and anybody interested in history or architecture will want to make a return visit.

The Walk

Leave the train/bus station area (1) and cross the road to the centre of the Plaça d'Espanya (2) with, in the centre, a huge statue of Jaime I, El Conqueridor (see notes, later, on the cathedral and also the introduction to this book). Go straight ahead through the Plaça de la Porta Pintada, then left into Carrer de Sant Miquel.

> The church on the corner (3), that of Santa Caterina de Sena (St Catherine of Siena) is now Russian Orthodox. If it is open, do go inside because it is so unusual – a rare and beautiful oasis in the heart of Catholic Mallorca.

Continue along Carrer de Sant Miquel and, when you reach Plaça de l'Olivar, make a short diversion to the left to view the **market building** (4).

> If you are early enough (usually 7am to 2pm) you can go inside and admire – or buy – the most wonderful flowers, fruit and vegetables.

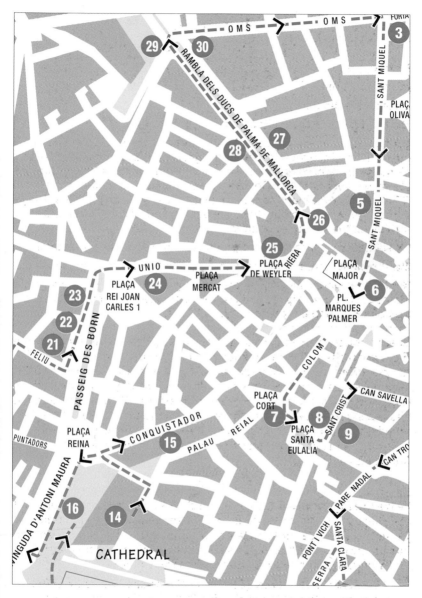

Continue along Sant Miquel and, on the left, you pass the church of **Sant Antoniet**, the cloister of which was restored by Banco Bilbao Vizcaya (BBVA) in 1979. Shortly after is the BBV building, and almost opposite, the church of **Sant Miquel** with elaborate stone carvings around its entrance.

A little further along, also on the right, is the **Museum of**

Contemporary Spanish Arts (5) – established by the Madrid-based Juan March Foundation

> In addition to temporary exhibits, there are permanent exhibitions of works by Picasso, Miró, Dalí and many other notable Spanish artists. Free entrance; open 10am to 6.30pm Mon-Fri, 10am to 2pm, closed on Sundays.

Continue in the same direction and enter the 19th-century **Plaça Mayor** (6).

> Almost every Spanish town and city has a Plaça Mayor, but this one is a bit different as it was built on the site of the building used by the Spanish Inquisition. Nowadays, the main square of Palma is attractively arcaded on all four sides with many excellent shops: a delightful place to wander around, protected from the summer sun. A craft market is held on Monday, Friday and Saturday.

Go straight across the square, walk through Plaça del Marques del Palmer and straight ahead into Carrer de Colom. Continue along this street for 200 metres and turn left at Plaça de Cort, noting the Baroque town hall and public library across to your right (7).

Having turned left, walk along Carrer de la Cadena and into **Plaça de Santa Eulalia** (8) with its large Gothic-style church – one of the oldest in Palma. Turn left after the entrance to the church and walk up Carrer del Sant Crist, passing – on your right – **El Bazar del Libro** (9), a fascinating second-hand bookshop. Take the second turn on your right into Carrer de Can Savellà.

> There are several attractive patios to admire along this pleasant street, including the Palacio Vivot on your right, regarded as the most important one. It was constructed in the 18th century, with arches and Corinthian columns adorning its spacious central courtyard. Visits can be arranged, tel: 971 721992.

At the end of this street, bear right towards Carrer de Can Troncoso, then right into Plaça de Sant Francesc and past the 13th-century church of **San Francisco** (10) on the left.

> Inside the church is the tomb of Ramon Llull – you'll find it at the far left-hand corner, behind the altar. The church is appropriately named after San Francisco because, as you will see, near to the main entrance there is a statue of Fray (Father/Friar) Junipero Serra – the diminutive but zealous Mallorcan missionary famous for his work in California (see Walk 10 for more details). For good or ill, he's got an indigenous native boy alongside him, before or after conversion. Open 9.30am to 1pm and 3.30pm to 6pm.

Continue in the same direction across the Plaça de Sant Francesc. Turn right into Carrer del Convent de Sant Francesc and then left along Carrer del Pare Nadal (after Jeronimo Nadal, a Mallorcan Jesuit priest). Go over a crossroads and, after a short distance, fork immediately left into Carrer de Santa Clara. Continue straight ahead to view the church of **Santa Clara** with its 13th-century cloister (11).

Go back from the church and take the second turn left into Carrer de Can Serra. After 100 metres pass, on the left, the 10th-century Banys Àrabs (12) or **Arab Baths**.

> The baths (open daily, €1.80, 2008) reflect the Moorish history of Mallorca. Although there are numerous fragments of Moorish remains throughout Palma, this is the only intact building open to the public (9.30am to 6pm). It is thought that the baths were part of a Moorish nobleman's house.

At the bottom of the street, turn right into Carrer de Can Formiguera and into a slightly wider area that includes the unremarkable College of Architects building. Turn left to pass through a gateway and then through the old city wall by way of the ancient gateway of **Porta de la Portella**. The lake that fronts the cathedral is now on your right.

> It is interesting to note that the lake was constructed after much of the seafront was reclaimed in the 1950s to construct the Paseo Maritimo (Passeig Maritim) running for 3km along the Bay of Palma.

Head left towards the sea, recalling that it wasn't always like this, and go slightly left up a wide flight of steps, then turn right to walk alongside the left-hand side of the lake – giving a superb view of the cathedral, reflected in the lake.

> The architects of the cathedral designed it to face seawards and the man-made lake mimics – very effectively – the original setting. You could, of course, have taken a short cut, but you would have missed the fabulous photo opportunity!

The cathedral

Stroll through the **Parc de la Mar** containing, at the westerly end, various contemporary sculptures (13). Continue to the end of the lake, turn right and go up the steps, passing an arch on your left and a man-made pool.

> The arch was, in Moorish times, an entrance to a shipyard – another indication of how much land has been reclaimed from the sea.

After a short distance, turn left up some steps and you arrive at the cathedral (14).

> A visit to the cathedral (*La Seu* in Mallorquin) is essential. Seasonal visiting hours, Monday to Saturday. Admission (2008) €4. Built on the site of a mosque, as was often the case, it measures 121 metres by 55 metres. Its origins can be traced to Jaime I, El Conqueridor (James I, The Conqueror) who ordered it to be built after surviving a fierce storm whilst on his way to invade Mallorca in 1229. The ensuing battle for Palma lasted for almost three months. Construction of the cathedral began in 1230 when the triumphant Jaime I returned home and left the job of running the island and building the cathedral in the hands of his son, Jaime II. It proved to be a bigger project than Jaime imagined, being interrupted by a succession of wars and plagues. It was basically finished in 1601 (though even now the bell tower is incomplete) and the result is one of the most impressive cathedrals in Europe. With its seaward profile and soaring pinnacled columns, the architecture has been described as "French Gothic" and has many interesting features, including the Puerta del Mar – the doorway facing the sea – and the main façade with its Renaissance-style entrance. The interior is constructed on a grand scale with 35 windows (including an enormous 11-metre-wide rose window), 18 side chapels and three naves. Behind the main altar, with its huge chandelier-like construction by Antoni Gaudí, are over 100 walnut choir-stalls. The tombs of both Jaime II and Jaime III can be found to the rear of the choir-stalls. You can also visit the Cathedral Treasury, replete with gold and silver monstrances (jewelled devotional objects), statues and other items.

Leaving the main cathedral entrance behind you, cross the Carrer de Palau Reial and turn right to pass in front of the **Almudaina Palace**, on your left, complete with sentry box outside its double doors that are surmounted by a coat of arms.

> The building dates from the 11th century, when it was both a Moorish fortress and palace. The Kings of Mallorca, starting with Jaime II in the 14th century also occupied it but it is now an official government residence used by King Juan Carlos when visiting the island. It includes the Museum of National Heritage. Opening hours are 10am to 7pm but closed Saturday afternoon and all day Sunday.

Turn left, noting, on the right, **Palau March**. Now a museum, this was built in the 1940s by the Mallorcan banker and philanthropist, Joan March. Turn left again and go down a flight of steps (Costa de la Seu).

Just here, there's the very pleasant Cappuccino Café – a convenient half-way place for coffee or a light lunch.

At the foot of the steps, or on leaving the café, turn right and make a there-and-back diversion along Carrer de Conquistador to admire the administrative buildings (15). Walk back and enter the top of the **S'Hort de Rei** – the King's Garden (16) – now a public park.

The park used to have several modern sculptures, including one by Joan Miró, but in 2008 there was just "Nancy" by the American sculptor (and inventor of the mobile) Alexander Calder. At the other end is a more recognisable piece: a representation of a hondero or Mallorcan sling thrower – 'Es Foner' – by Lorenzo Rossello.

The Balearic islands were once called the "Isles of the Slingers" in honour of their 15,000-year-old traditional use of slings as defensive and offensive weapons. Many early would-be invaders of Mallorca were deterred as the stones hurled by slingers could easily overcome both swordsmen and archers. Their use declined in medieval times with the development of more sophisticated weaponry, but sling-throwing has been revived in recent years as a competitive sport on the island.

Just behind the sling-thrower, there's an entrance to a quiet area with an ornamental pond, with an unusual view of the Almudaina Palace. Have a break here, then leave the gardens and turn right to cross over Avengida d'Antoni Maura. In the middle of the busy junction, look – on your left – for the statue of **Ramon Llull** (17).

Ramon Llull, the celebrated 13th-century Mallorcan mystic and philosopher, was the son of an upper-class Aragonese family. He became a hermit, made pilgrimages to Rome, Santiago and Jerusalem and established the monastery of Miramar between Deià and Valldemosa. He attempted to combine aspects of mysticism, poetry and philosophy and was also reputed to be an alchemist. Life for Ramon was, however, never smooth: he was stoned to death in Tunisia by the Moslems he was trying to convert.

Continue along this road, Passeig de Sagrera. After Plaça de la Llotja, the pleasant square on your right, you pass the ornate 15th-century Gothic masterpiece of **La Llotja** (being renovated in 2008). This used to be Palma's commercial exchange, where merchants traded jewels, silver, silk and spices. La Llotja is only open to the public when exhibitions take place inside the building. The street you are walking along is named after Guillermo Sagrera who designed both La Llotja and the Portal del Mirador of the cathedral (see earlier).

You then pass the impressive civic buildings replete with flags and cannons on your right. At the next junction, turn right into the Carrer de Consulat to pass between what are now government buildings into the attractive **Plaça de la Drassana** (18).

The first building that you pass on your right used to be the offices of the Merchant Shipping Tribunal. In the centre of the square, there is a statue of Jaime Ferrer, a celebrated 14th-century Mallorcan mariner. In the 17th century, this area was under water, being the site of an important Palma shipyard.

Head out of the square, uphill, cross Carrer dels Apuntadors (noted for its restaurants) then head to the right into Carrer del Forn de la Gloria. The first large house on your right is **Cal Capitá Flexes** (19), built by a wealthy 17th-century seafarer and trader. After passing the side street of Carrer de Can Boneo on your left, turn left into Carrer de Montenegro. On the left, look for the house called **Ca'n Montenegro** (20) with a large stone plaque between the two doorways.

In the 17th century, Ca'n Montenegro belonged to one of the Grand Masters of the Knights of Malta, one of Palma's most important (and wealthiest)groups of citizens. The Knights of Malta, originally the Knights of the Order of St John of Jerusalem, were originally empowered to provide amenities to pilgrims and crusaders. This was not sufficient to satisfy the more ambitious members, who soon saw opportunities for themselves as upper-class pirates. They had a stroke of luck when the Hapsburg emperor Charles V ceded the strategically-important Maltese islands to them in 1530. They then became ever more powerful, with Ottoman shipping seen as a legitimate prime target and their increased wealth enabled the Grand Masters to acquire expensive houses in Malta and elsewhere in the Mediterranean, including Mallorca. They were ejected from Malta in 1798 after a French invasion of the island – and the party ended.

Continue along Carrer de Montenegro to a T-junction. Turn right here, along Carrer de Sant Feliu and soon you will see what used to be the small 13th-century Gothic chapel of **Sant Feliu**, now a private art gallery (21). At the end of Sant Feliu, turn left (at a taxi rank and small palm trees) into the Passeig des Born.

It seems hard to believe but this fashionable street was only reclaimed from the sea in the 17th century. A river bed carried floodwaters down its centre, like many of the 'torrents' that you will find on your walks in the rest of Mallorca.

Continue along the Passeig de Born until you pass, on your left, **Casal Solleric** (22) – an elegant 18th-century building now used for exhibitions (free entrance). Shortly after this, turn right at the **Plaça del Rei Joan Carles I** (23).

Continue into Carrer de la Unio and soon you are in **Plaça del Mercat** with its impressive and unusual architectural features on your right. Make a short diversion to the large church of **San Nicolas** (24) across the square and to your right.

Continue along Carrer de la Unio, which becomes **Plaza de Weyler**. There are several interesting buildings along here – on your left, you cannot miss the magnificent balconied art nouveau building that was once the **Gran Hotel** (25).

The Gran Hotel was designed by the modernist architect Lluis Dòmenich I Montaner and it opened its doors in 1903 as a luxury hotel. After a change of use to an administrative centre in 1942, the building began to deteriorate. Fortunately, it has been restored by the La Caixa financial institution. It reopened in 1993 as the "Caixa Forum", comprising an art gallery, café bar (an excellent place to relax) and exhibition hall.

The **Teatre Principal** is at the end of this street, on the opposite side from the old Gran Hotel. From here, turn left, along Carrer de la Riera and left again, and you will be greeted by the incongruous sight of a large, chunky, modern sculpture near to a pair of Roman centurions (26). You are now at the bottom of **La Rambla** – a city boulevard with trees and flower sellers along its entire length, reminiscent of the street of the same name in Barcelona. Cross the road and walk up the middle of La Rambla. Half-way along, on your right, you pass the church (27) of **Santa Teresa de Jesus** (1624) and, almost opposite, a row of sympathetically restored balconied buildings (28).

At the top of La Rambla, with the **Centre Cultural de la Misericordia** (29) on your left and Via Roma straight ahead, turn right into Carrer dels Oms (30). At the end of the pedestrianised street, you come to a crossroads – and you're back at the Russian Orthodox church of **Santa Caterina** (3) on the right. Continue ahead to pass through the **Plaça d'Espanya** (2) and cross the road to the station, where there's a bar if you have a long wait for the train or bus.

Other places to visit

Bellver Castle: 3km from the centre of Palma. The building dates from the 14th century and has served as a royal residence, a prison and a mint. It now houses a museum and a collection of Roman sculptures. Open every day, €1.80 (2008).

Poble Espanyol (Pueblo Español): the "Spanish Village" created between 1965 and 1967 by Fernando Chueca Goitia on the western outskirts of Palma, depicting the development of Spanish architecture. Several reproductions of famous palaces and other locations from all over Spain: 73 monuments, 15 streets and 12 squares together with craft shops and cafés.

2. Banyalbufar
Terraces above the sea

Grade: moderate – but with a strenuous climb at the beginning

Distance: 5km

Time: 2hrs

Start & Finish: the town hall at the centre of Banyalbufar

How to get there: Ma-10 from Valldemossa or Andratx directions. Large, free (in 2008) car park about 400m from the village centre, in the Estellencs/Andratx direction.

Map: IGN 670/III (see reference chart in introduction)

Checklist: walking boots; water; picnic; camera

Banyalbufar, a village of about 500 permanent inhabitants, was originally 'Banyalbahar', Arabic for 'new settlement close to the sea'. Three wide valleys and its many terraces, irrigated by a system of water channels and storage tanks, have contributed to its agricultural past when cereals, olives and, most important, grapes were grown in vast quantities. The village was famous for its Malmsey dessert wine but the vines that produced the Malvasia grape were destroyed by the 1891 outbreak of *Phylloxera*, which affected the whole island. Subsequently, tomatoes as well as olives and almonds were cultivated. Today, many of the old terraces are being restored with traditional crops and – best news of all – wine is being produced again: in 1995, the Malvasia de Banyalbufar co-op was formed and recently produced over 6,000 litres of prize-winning wines. One of Banyalbufar's more unexpected products was cement: it was produced in large quantities in the 1940s from the surrounding limestone, but the factory is now in ruins. Tourism has become a more important part of the village economy, with three hotels and several bars and restaurants.

The GR221 Problem

The Banyalbufar walk in the first edition of this book can not be completed because the owner of Es Rafal has obtained a court ruling to close his property to walkers – even though the traditional path through it has been walked for decades and, even more importantly, includes a key section of the GR221 route which was established just a few years ago. To put it into context, this is comparable to closing a lengthy section of the Pennine Way in the UK or the GR10 in France at the request of a property owner: it just would not happen. To make matters worse, the authorities have erected a board apologising for the closure, but without any suggestion as to what walkers should do to complete the GR221. It is a disgraceful situation – but luckily there is a circular walk that avoids the problem!

The New Walk

Because of the GR221 closure, I have had to find a replacement for the one that used the Es Rafal route. The new route is based on Walk 10 by Pat Robinson in the "Guide to Banyalbufar" booklet, revised 2000 and available in the village. I have put more flesh on the description and generally updated it to produce what I feel is a very worthwhile replacement. Before starting, get in the mood by having a coffee or beer – I recommend the Café Bellavista because of its terrace with sea views. Afterwards, call in at the Casa de la Vila (town hall) where the friendly staff have a selection of maps and guides (though mostly in Mallorquin/Catalan). Have a moan about the GR221 at the same time.

1.   Start in the main square, Plaça de la Vila. Go to the left of the town hall and walk up Carrer Jeromi Alberti. Ignore the enticing stepped track on the right after 5mins or so and the prominent red paint mark and steps after 10mins.

2.   Continue walking steeply uphill – in the springtime there are masses of poppies to admire. You soon pass a large water *deposito*

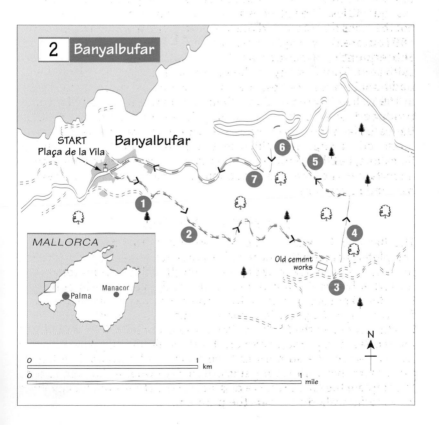

(reservoir) on the left **(15mins)**. Ignore a right fork and go downhill for a short way before climbing again.

3. After about **30 mins** you will see an electricity pylon and cables about 50m to your left. So that you are sure that this really is where you should be, you should see a concrete track to your right, a 'Coto Privado de Caza' sign nailed to a tree, also on the right, and a steel gate leading to a walled track on your left. Fork left onto this track and close and bolt the gate.

4. Having passed through the gateway, continue between the stone walls, passing the derelict house noted by Pat Robinson – though it no longer has a house number and it looks as though it could collapse completely quite soon.

   The path winds downhill and around the head of an attractive valley, passing a renovated farmstead and a small *casita* **(45mins)**. The owners have renovated the buildings and restored the terraces in this delightful hidden valley. Numerous fruit trees have also been planted to complement the traditional crops.

5. Continue downhill on the main track through holly oak, pine and

Buildings and terraces in the 'hidden valley'

cistus, ignoring tracks to left or right. Go through a gateway **(55mins)** and pass a stone shelter as the scenery changes abruptly to olive groves, with excellent views of Banyalbufar to the left.

6. At the main road, turn left **(1hr 5mins)** into an area with a recycling facility and two football pitches. Walk around the

pitches to the far corner of the second pitch where you will find, perhaps after a little searching, a rough path that goes through a gap in the bushes and immediately turns left downhill with a wire fence on the right. It soon becomes a nicely stepped track that must have been a mule route to the village – just as the descent from Es Rafal was. Let's hope that this one is not closed as well!

7. The path joins a tarmac crossroads (**1hr 15mins**) with Ca'n Pelut on the right. Cross straight over and continue downhill. Turn left at the main road and continue for about 800m to the centre of the village. This final section is along the main road, and the first 400m or so does not have a pavement, so take care.

Other walks in the area

The best source of walks is the inexpensive "Guide to Banyalbufar" booklet mentioned previously and available locally. Directions are sketchy, but it includes plenty of ideas for walks, including the bare bones of this route. It also includes an excellent potted history of the village. Profits are used to support cultural activities for young people of Banyalbufar, so please buy a copy.

Places of interest

The **Torre d'Es Verger** is near the 88.6km marker on the road to Estellencs. This ancient defensive tower (also known as the Tower of Ses Animes) is a popular viewpoint. Sunsets from here are unforgettable. **Esporles** is a nice small town 6km west of Banyalbufar, with an authentic unspoilt feel. **Valldemossa** is easily reached by bus or car: busy in the daytime, but pleasantly quiet in the evening – see Walk 26. The nearby **Port d'Es Canonge** has an attractive harbour and two restaurants serving locally-caught fish.

3. S'Arracó to Sa Trapa
The Wild West of Mallorca

Grade: moderate

Distance: 10.5km or 14km

Time: 6 hours or 7 hours

Start & Finish: the main square (Plaza de Toledo) in S'Arracó

How to get there: S'Arracó is 2km west of the town of Andratx. There are regular buses from Andratx or Sant Elm to S'Arracó

Map: IGN 697/II (1:25,000 – see reference chart in introduction)

Checklist: walking boots; water; picnic; camera

Notes: one of the alternative endings to this walk involves a short bus journey – if you intend to do this, take money.

The walk to the ruins of Sa Trapa monastery from either S'Arracó or Sant Elm is deservedly popular. This version starts from the town of S'Arracó and I am indebted to my guides Sally and Graham Beale, who live in this attractive village, and whom I first met by chance on the slopes of the Galatzó mountain!

The Walk

From the Plaza de Toledo in S'Arracó, walk up the main street (i.e. in the direction of Andratx). Pass the Restaurant Puput (Mallorquin for Hoopoe, an exotic-looking but fairly common bird in Mallorca) and turn left down Carrer del Porvenir.

1. Follow this tarmac lane as it slopes uphill. Turn left **(10 mins)** at Barri sa Clota and then keep left at a fork **(15 mins)**. After a further five minutes, fork right, following the power and telephone cables.

2. Continue uphill and pass Ca'n Corso (no. 33) – a white house on your right. Soon **(30 mins)** you reach a T-junction.

3. Go left here and walk through a mountain pass **(45 mins)** overlooking a beautiful valley. The path runs alongside terraced cultivation and you soon reach the head of the valley **(1hr)**. Go left here, past some sparse trees.

    There would be more trees here, were it not for a fire that ravaged the area in the mid-1990s. Nowadays you will see less evidence of this disaster – thanks to regrowth and planting of young trees.

4. The path contours around the hillside until **(1hr 15mins)** you come to a fork marked with a cairn and both red and yellow waymarks. It is *very* important that you find this fork.

5. Having found the fork that marks the start of the path, turn right

The island of Dragonera from the threshing circle of Sa Trapa

downhill, following occasional yellow paint marks. Just two minutes after joining the path, turn left at a cairn and the yellow paint marks take you into a deep valley with a dam on your right.

Our walking group conjectured that this is to control flash floods. Any other suggestions?

6. Turn left into the valley (**1hr 30mins**) and walk away from the dam along a wide, stony track. Continue uphill, passing an impressive variety of flowers in the spring including pink cistus, purple thistle, speedwell – and newly planted saplings that should help to regenerate the valley.

7. Go left at a T-junction (**1hr 45mins**). A trig point is passed and views soon open up along the coast towards Estellencs and Banyalbufar. The path curves around the hillside and soon your route is waymarked with red dots and arrows.

8. At a T-junction (**2hrs 5mins**) head to the right on a path (red waymarks) between the ever-present rosemary and cistus. Just two minutes later, go right at the next T-junction and you are on a well-walked, popular track.

Enjoy a 15-minute break here – time for lunch!

Continue along the obvious track, enjoying an excellent view of the island of Dragonera.

The island is now a nature reserve but, just a few years ago, it came close to being sold off as a hotel development! Its name is said to be derived either from its dragon-like shape or perhaps from the lizards that inhabit the island.

After lunch, work your way down the once-wooded hillside. Very soon (**2hrs 50mins**) you begin to approach the terraces that were cultivated by the monks of Sa Trapa . A wide track winds down to the old monastery.

9. You approach the Sa Trapa monastery complex just after a tiled channel on your right (**3hrs 30mins**).

    This is part of an irrigation system for the terraces – the Christian monks were greatly indebted to their Moorish predecessors. Make a short diversion alongside this channel, climb a flight of steps and you will see a small reservoir. Beyond this, a stone archway leads to a 10-metre tunnel with a freshwater spring at the far end. We have allowed 15 minutes for this diversion.

    A further half hour has been allowed to explore the ruins of Sa Trapa. Volunteer workers from GOB ("Balearic Group for Ornithology and the Defence of Nature" – a conservation group that deserves your support) have started to restore the buildings after many years of neglect. Take time to walk along to the threshing circle, passing the restored mill, which has a geared system of grinding wheels. As a bonus, there is a fabulous view of Dragonera from the threshing circle – both this and the mill were donkey-powered. Web sites about Sa Trapa include the relevant part of the official GOB site, www.gobmallorca.com/trapa/index.htm (only in Mallorquin at present) and www.baleares.com/promo.php4?id=359&elem=n&canal=19 (in English). The Trappist order is a branch of the Cistercians; it was founded in 1660 by Dominique de Rancé, a priest in the Cistercian abbey of La Trappe. Dominique obviously thought that the Cistercians were getting a bit soft and he introduced a regime of hard labour, silence and a diet of bread and vegetables. Even worse, wine was also forbidden. Not surprisingly, there are not many Trappists about nowadays.

Return to the main track (**4hrs 15mins** including the diversion and visit to Sa Trapa) and turn right with the sign pointing to "Sant Elm 1hr". Walk to the end of the headland and turn left at two trees, keeping them on your left. **From here, pay careful attention for the safest descent:** look for a large red dot on a rock and then walk around to the right of it. Scramble down from here to the next red dot, then go left and down some rock steps – you are now heading to the right. Keep close to the rocks on your right and, at a gap with several dwarf palms, again go to the right over a large boulder to yet another red dot. From here, do *not* turn left. Instead, follow the steps and paint dots all the way down to join a clear path.

The smaller island, soon to be seen ahead, is Pantaleu.

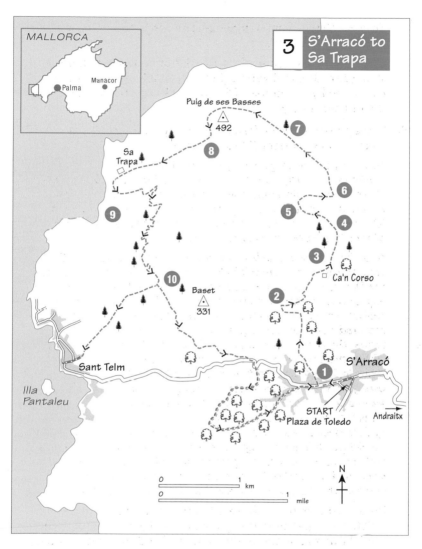

MALLORCA

Manacor

Palma

Puig de ses Basses

△ 492

7

8

Sa Trapa

6

9

5

4

3

Ca'n Corso

10

Baset

△ 331

2

Sant Telm

S'Arracó

Illa Pantaleu

1

START
Plaza de Toledo

Andraitx

N

0 ———— 1 km

0 ———— 1 mile

10. At an obvious junction **(4hrs 45mins)** you have three choices:

a. Turn right, between the pillars, to Cala Bissett. This is an unlikely choice unless you want a really long walk and can organise transport back to the start.

b. Go straight on to Sant Elm. This takes 25 minutes and passes a small house on the way. A notice board shows routes from Sant Elm to La Trapa and other destinations. Continue to the north end of Sant Elm. If you feel like even more walking, there is a pleasant route around the headland from Sant Elm to S'Arracó. Otherwise, make your way towards the beach and find the time of the next bus (every two hours) or telephone for a taxi (very reasonably priced).

c. As a final option, you can skip Sant Elm and walk to S'Arracó. This takes about an hour. Turn left at the junction and, just 2 minutes later, turn left along Camí Punta de Sa Galera. A little later **(5hrs 5mins)** join the Camí sa Font dels Morers. Continue on this wide track, ignoring all side turnings, until you join the main road, where you turn left **(5hrs 25mins)**.

Walk down the winding road and, just before the crash barrier on your right (and some 100 metres before the cemetery on your left), turn right along a trac, Barri son Tió. This passes a tumbledown house – note that occasional yellow paint marks indicate your route. It may seem as though this is taking you away from S'Arracó – but don't panic: after 5 minutes, fork left downhill (yellow paint marks) and, after another 5 minutes, join a tarmac road. Turn left here and follow the tarmac all the way to the main road, where you turn right and walk the short distance to S'Arracó and your starting point, after about 6 hours including all stops.

Other walks in the area

See Walk 4 which also includes details of a walks leaflet.

Places of interest

S'Arracó is a pleasant village; its parish church, dating from 1742, has a statue of the "Our Lady of la Trapa". **Andratx**, the administrative centre, is 2km east of S'Arracó. It has a 13th-century church, dedicated to Santa María de Andratx, and a hugely impressive town hall. The port of Andratx, 4km away, has a yacht marina and several restaurants.

Another worthwhile trip is from Sant Elm to **Dragonera** – visit www.conselldemallorca.cat/dragonera for information about the island. A small boat leaves every hour or so. On the island there is an information centre, several waymarked trails and abundant birdlife. Be sure to tell the boatman what time you intend to return – and check the time of the last boat!

4. Cap d'es Llamp and S'Atalaya

A short excursion from Paguera or Port d'Andraitx

Grade: moderate

Distance: 7km (approx.10km if starting from the centre of the port)

Time: 2 to 3 hrs

Start & Finish: entrance to residential development approx 1.5km south-west of Port d'Andraitx. See below for access by foot or car

How to get there: drive to the port area, the follow directions below. Plenty of buses to the port.

Map: IGN 697/IV (1:25,000 – see reference chart in introduction)

Checklist: walking boots; water; picnic; camera

As elsewhere in Mallorca, access on foot is constantly changing. In this case, the start of the walk begins with a "Prohibido el Paso" and a private property sign. Nevertheless, the walk is a popular one, is well waymarked and described in a local walks leaflet – so enjoy it while you can – before some property developer locks the gates!

The Walk

From the port of Andratx, walk or drive for 500m up to Carrer Garcia Murago, signed to Camp de Mar. At a roundabout, keep right signed to Cala Llamp. Go uphill to the next roundabout and take the third exit up Carrer Orada. After 300m keep straight ahead up Carrer Pagel (do not turn right into a continuation of C/Orada). After 400m, turn left into Carrer Anfos and after 200m or so you reach the end of the road: double-gated, with "Prohibido el Paso", "private property" and even "big game" warning signs. Nevertheless, this is the start of a popular local walk so park your car securely and follow these instructions:

1. Go through a gap on either side of the (quite-likely locked) gates and walk along the road that serves the properties on the headland. Reassuringly, pass a cairn **(7mins)**.

2. A few minutes later pass a large red marker – ignore this. Continue along the road, passing occasional cairns to a bench, a cairn – and a second pair of locked gates **(20mins).** These were new to me in 2007 – a wealthy but mean-spirited part-time resident has blocked access to the headland and you are faced with a choice. Unless things have changed again, you may notice that the wire fence on the right of the gate has been cut through by determined walkers, so you may feel inclined to pass through the gap. If you decide to do so then, after a couple of minutes of walking, you should be able to find a red marker cross on the right of the track.

3. From this marker, follow a cairned path to the triangulation point on the headland of Cap des Llamp. Retrace your steps to the fence

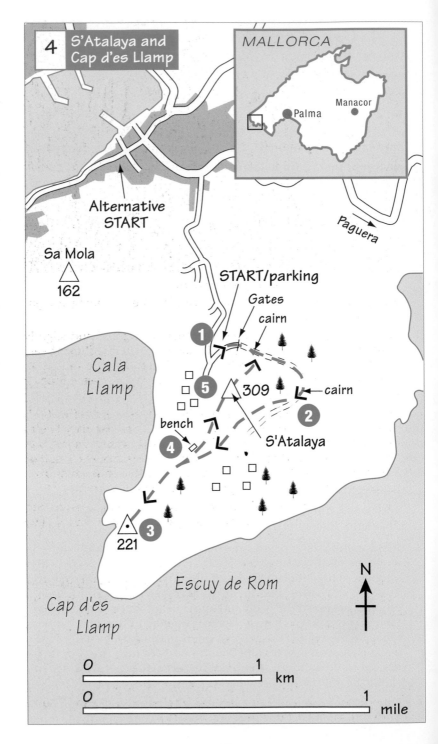

4 S'Atalaya and Cap d'es Llamp

MALLORCA

Manacor
Palma

Paguera

Alternative START

Sa Mola
162

START/parking
Gates
cairn
1
cairn
Cala Llamp
5
309
2
bench
4
S'Atalaya
3
221

Escuy de Rom

Cap d'es Llamp

N

0   1   km
0   1 mile

Cala Llamp from Atalaya

and pass the bench seen earlier **(40mins)** before going straight ahead to ascend Atalaya.

4. Start the ascent on a cairned path that goes uphill and slightly right. After a minute or so, take the path (also cairned) that bears slightly left as this gives better views. Eventually you reach the summit (306m on my GPS, 309m on the map – close enough!) marked by a wooden cross.

5. Storms have felled many trees and the descent was not (in 2007) obvious. This seemed best: start to descend an imaginary line at 90° to the ascent – you will be facing a bay (marked on maps as Escuy de Rom), heading SE and will have your back to the broadest part of the cross. After a couple of minutes you start to follow a series of cairns that soon begin to mark a well-used path.

   After 15 minutes you hit the outward road at the cairn mentioned at point 1. Turn left here, back to the gates and, if you arrived by car, your parking place.

Other walks in the area

A free leaflet of sketch maps "10 Excursions a peu per Andratx" may still be available from information offices in Andraitx and Port d'Andraitx. Destinations (mostly involving linear walks) include Sant Elm, Camp de Mar and Sa Trapa. In 2007, all that the tourist office in Ardratx could offer was a photocopied sheet of maps.

Places of interest

The inland town of **Andratx** is worth a visit – be sure to view the magnificent civic offices and gardens. **Estellencs** and **Banyalbufar** are both a short drive along the coastal road.

5. Galatzó
Mallorca's Matterhorn

Grade: strenuous

Distance: 12km, plus 990m of ascent.

Time: at least 7 hours

Start & Finish: roadside near the sports centre (Poliesportiu Municipal), Puigpunyent village centre

How to get there: from Palma and the east, use the Via Cintura and follow signs to Puigpunyent. From resorts west of Palma, drive through Calvià and then north-east to join the road from Palma. There are local buses and, according to the Puigpunyent web site, the great-great-grandfather of the present operator first established public transport service in 1808, using a donkey and cart.

Map: IGN 698/I (1:25,000 – see reference chart in introduction)

Checklist: walking boots; water; picnic; camera

Notes: parking is fairly easy in Puigpunyent, being off the tourist route. The sports centre (Poliesportiu Municipal) is signed from the village and, as it is easy to find, this is the start of the walk.

Puigpunyent (on some maps, 'Puigpuñent') dates from the 13th century, being created after the Spanish conquest of Mallorca. Situated in a fertile valley within the Tramuntana range, it is surrounded by mountains, the most famous being Galatzó.

Galatzó stands on its own: a striking landscape feature, visible from miles away. From a distance, it looks an impossible challenge, but the route is well-graded with a variety of paths and waymarked tracks. It is very popular with locals – on a January day a few years ago, there were at least 50 young people on the summit, enjoying a picnic. However, this is a strenuous walk with 990m (3300ft) of ascent, and you must allow enough daylight time for its completion – as I did not do on New Year's Day 2007. My friend John Handley and I had to walk back to our car in Puigpunyent by moonlight, using the light from a mobile phone to read the map. A couple of navigational errors did not help!

The Walk

Walk uphill from the sports centre in the direction of Esporles (road un-named in 2007, but signed signed as the Ma-1101).

1. Just before the 1km marker post (and next to the Puigpunyent sign) where the road bends right, keep straight on to a tarmac lane, Carretera Nova d'Estellencs. After 100m go through an entrance with signs prohibiting cars and motor bikes. Eventually, the lane curves left and passes below the huge Son Forteza property **(25 min)**. Just after a left hairpin, turn right on a track with a

waymark for Camí Vell D'Estellencs. This avoids the original route past the farm buildings. The path zigzags uphill, goes through a gap with a rickety bedstead gate (Mallorcans often use old bedsteads as gates) then right onto a wide forest track, winding uphill.

Son Forteza dates from the late 17th century. Prince Charles stayed here during a visit to Mallorca in 1990.

2. Follow a wide forest track, winding uphill. Pass a farm building **(50 mins)** above and on the left. The track curves sharply to the left then a new track, marked by a cairn and a red dot, forks to the right. After 20 metres, turn right again. A few minutes later you come to an intersection of four tracks. Go uphill – almost straight ahead – on a wide track marked by a red dot on a rock on your left. Ignore the tracks to your left and right.

    Continue along the obvious track and pass through a gateway in a stone wall **(1 hr)** and turn right. Continue uphill and bear right

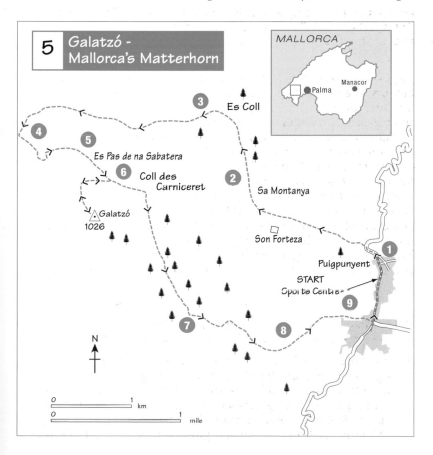

(**1hr 10min**) on a forest track, following the red dots to a T-junction (**1hr 20min**) with signpost pointing right to Es Grau and Puigpunyent and left to Galatzó. Be sure to take the left turn and head uphill, still with occasional red dots.

Amazingly this appears to be used by mountain bikers. I spotted a helmet, but no biker. More commonly, there are wild boar (jabali) in abundance. Loads of evidence from scrapings and noises that sounded like creaking gates. I never saw one, but felt those piggy eyes watching me.

3. Continue uphill, ignoring side turnings and soon the path levels out and you reach a wall where you climb over a wooden ladder stile next to a locked steel gate (**1hr 45min**).

Take a 10-minute break and admire the view. Leaving the ladder stile behind you, turn left and follow the path downhill for about 200 metres. Where the track starts to bend to the right (**2hr 10min**), fork left on a path marked by a small cairn and a red arrow on a tree. It is very important that you take this path otherwise you will drop down into the valley and get hopelessly lost! Very soon (**2hrs 15mins**) there are coastal views and then you see Galatzó, straight ahead.

The sight is breathtaking! You may wonder how you will ever get to the top, but it really is only a couple of hours from here – a memorable climb with wonderful views along the way.

The path undulates around the hillside, passing (**2hrs 25mins**) a circular stone construction – possibly the remains of a *sitja*. The path heads downhill (**2hrs 30mins**) – losing a fair chunk of height already gained – soon leading through a gap in the wall. Head to the right and into a small valley.

4. Continue across the head of the valley, keeping to the main track. Storms have felled an enormous number of trees here but, despite a bit of weaving about, the track is still fairly clear.

Pass a stone water trough (**2hr 35min**), keep slightly left and follow occasional red dots then bear left (**2hr 40min**) at a point where there is a large gap in the wall to your right. This cuts a few metres off the 'official' route. (The wooden sign off to the right reassuringly points uphill to Galatzó!)

5. The path now zigzags steeply uphill. At **2hr 50min**, pass a *sitja* on the left and another Galatzó sign. Follow the stony uphill path to arrive (**3hr 20min**) at the right-hand end of a limestone ridge. A signpost points right to Pas d'es Cossi and left to Galatzó.

Take a 15-minute break here – it's a pleasant place and there's a makeshift bench in a shady spot.

Galatzó from near to point 6

Continue in the 'Puig de Galatzó' direction. Occasional waymarks take you towards the main massif.

6. At the top of a pass you reach a point where there were, until a few years ago, the ruins of a small building but you'll now find just the outlines of its foundations. You are now at the Pas de na Sabatera **(3hrs 50mins)** where you turn right for the final assault on Galatzó. Follow the cairns steeply uphill, then turn right to gain the west of the ridge. Continue following the cairns along a winding path with occasional gullies.

    You reach a clearing – look uphill from here and you will see a rock face with, "CRISTO" painted on it. In 2007 this had faded but was still legible – as were other inscriptions, including a website address! Climb straight up (an arrow points the way) but, just over half way up, note the arrow pointing right to a cairn on the skyline. The peak – with triangulation point, is soon visible. Swing left to reach the summit **(4hrs 25mins)**.

    Take a break for 20 minutes – admire (and photograph) the view of Palma and the mountains all around you.

7. Retrace your descent – with care – back to the Pas de na Sabatera **(5hrs 10mins)** and turn right to continue along the main track. Cross scree slopes **(5hr 20min)** and then climb up and over two rocky outcrops, the second – marked with a couple of small cairns – being Coll des Carniceret.

Start descending toward the tall lookout tower and shelter but, about 100m before the tower, there's a wire fence. Just before this, turn right – downhill – and follow the occasional green paint marks **(5hr 45min)**.

7. Just 10 minutes later, go right at a waymark post, then left to continue downhill. At a Y-junction **(6hrs)** fork right downhill and five minutes later, at a T-junction, turn left – yes, I know there's a painted arrow on the road pointing to the right, but you *must* turn left here.

    Continue along this road, ignoring all turns to left or right and you reach a major junction by a house, with a sign on the right to "La Reserva" adventure centre. As we've had enough adventures for today, turn **left** here **(6hr 10min)**.

    Continue a lengthy trudge passing a left fork **(6hr 45min)** where we keep to the right on the more obvious road (the left fork leads to houses).

9. Finally **(7hr 10min)** hit the main road, Carretera de Galilea and turn left, soon entering Puigpunyent and passing a church on your left.

    There are a couple of bars before you reach the centre of the village and your car.

Other walks in the area

La Reserva (mentioned above) offers various activities, from walks to rock climbing and very much more; see: www.lareservaaventur.com. The next walk, from Galilea to Bauza and Son Font is a popular one, giving excellent views of Galatzó on the return to Galilea.

Places of interest

Puigpunyent has several bars and restaurants, but is mainly residential. Galilea and Calvià are nearby and worth a visit – see next walk. The newer development of Son Serralta is 2km from Puigpunyent, on the Palma road.

6. Galilea, Bauza and Son Font
Valley views – and a mountain panorama

Grade: easy (if not climbing Bauza)

Distance: 6km (Son Font, return) or 4km (Bauza, return) or 8km (Son Font, Bauza and back to Galilea)

Time: 2 to 3 hours

Start & Finish: Galilea village centre

How to get there: From Palma and all resorts to the west, drive to Calvià, then to Capdellà, and head north-east on the road to Galilea. From the north, approach via Puigpunyent and you will see Bauza on your left. In Galilea, park near to the church, in the centre of the village.

Map: IGN 698/III and 698/IV (1:25,000) or just 698 (1:50,000) – see reference chart in introduction

Checklist: walking boots; water; picnic; camera

Galilea is on the slopes of Galatzó, at an altitude of about 450 metres. The route takes you across a beautiful wooded valley to Son Font (above Calvià) and back again; the views are very different in each direction. Starting from Calvià entails a relentless uphill slog on tarmac – take a taxi instead. Maps suggest that the area to the east of our route, towards Coma de S'Aigua, might be useful for a circular walk, but this has so far proved impossible.

For those who fancy some additional exertion, there's an optional climb up Galilea's mini-mountain of Bauza (marked on maps as Puig de na Bauçà) with some spectacularly beautiful views from the top.

The Walk

Before setting off, be sure to admire the views from this beautiful village and visit the 13th-century church of the Immaculate Conception. A church was first built on this site in 1238 but the present building is mainly 19th century. Note that there is a bar/restaurant next to the church offering typical Mallorcan tapas and strong coffee, should you need sustenance before the walk. There is also a hostel just around the corner run by two very friendly nuns. They can provide a bed for the night and would be pleased to cook you a three-course meal.

1. Follow the road from Galilea towards Puigpunyent. About a hundred metres down this road there is a shrine carved into the rocks which is being cared for by the local community. Continue down the road until you reach a gate that marks the start of your path. This is between the 8.3km and 8.4km marker posts.

   At this point there are two gates, one marked as the private road to the Son Cortey estate and the other – the one you need – has a ladder to climb over. A sign indicates that dogs are not allowed.

2. Follow the track along a gentle incline up and to the right. This track is in regular use by workers, possibly for the Mallorcan equivalent of the Forestry Commission. As you walk along the path there are good views of Galilea and down to the sea.

3. After about 10 minutes, there is a track off to the right – this is the parting of the ways. You can **either** continue more or less on the level to Son Font, **or** you can climb Bauza.

Looking back towards Bauza from near to Son Font

The Walk to Son Font

Taking the track to the right, mentioned above, continue towards Son Font. This track is narrower and a little rocky but affords beautiful views over the countryside and ravines. Following the path is easy, as people have left marks to indicate the route. Much of the path is through trees, which give some protection from the sun.

4. Eventually **(40 mins)** you will see a track to the right, leading to a small stone building. Ignore this and continue south, along the meandering path. As the path starts to climb directly towards the Son Font development, you have a choice of routes – a pleasant long loop to the left, or a more direct one favoured by walkers in a hurry. You can use one on the outward route and the other on the way back.

5. At the end of the stony track, pass through a gap to the right of iron gates **(1 hour)** and you're on a tarmac road that leads between the super-mansions of Son Font.

   You now have to decide whether to walk back to Galilea or down the tarmac road to Calvià, which will take almost an hour. If you decide to do this, ignore all side turns until you reach the town. Unless there is a car waiting for you at Son Font or Calvià, take a taxi back to Galilea.

   If you decide to walk back to Galilea, do be careful not to turn left towards the building noted in point (4) – just head north with Galatzó ahead and Bauza to the right.

The Bauza Excursion

These instructions continue from point 3, above.

Continue up a little further and follow a track off to the left to Bauza (there is a sign in the tree but the name has almost worn off). The track gets a little steeper but is still not difficult. On the way up there are two round structures each about 3 or more metres across and perhaps 5 metres high. Given the amount of limestone around, these must be old lime kilns.

Further up the track, pause to admire an excellent view of Galilea and note the two stone shelters, both in very good condition.

6. You reach a clearing **(40 mins)** – an opportunity for a 10-minute break before the climb to the top of Bauza. The path moves off to the left and is easy to follow into the trees. It soon gets narrower and becomes stepped. This last section is a bit of a slog but well worth it when you get to the top **(1 hour),** a height of 614 metres, and see the magnificent 360° views.

7. To return, retrace your steps down Bauza to point (3) and walk back to Galilea, which will take you less than an hour.

A scouting connection

During my final reconnaissance for this book, I ran out of time – partly by my ill-conceived plan to walk from Calvià to Galilea. I am greatly indebted to Stephen Baggaley, who lives in Mallorca, and helped me to complete the groundwork by turning a reconnoitre into a project for his scout group. They celebrated by cooking pancakes on top of Bauza – what a great idea!

Other walks in the area

A free booklet "Landscapes of Calvià" is available from information centres in resorts. This includes three walks in the area of Calvià town.

Places of interest

Calvià (www.calvia.com) has an interesting church and the prospect of cold drinks. There is also a town hall, but don't go there expecting any help with excursions, as the information service has been "devolved" to the coastal resorts. Near the church, there is a school of music with an excellent mural depicting the history of Mallorca. **Puigpunyent** is four kilometres north of Galilea. Famed for the nearby Puig de Galatzó (see previous walk) it is also notable for its prehistoric sites, including the talayots of Son Burguet and Son Serralta – see the main introduction in this book for information on talayots.

Our favourite beach: see Walk 12

East & North-East

7. Pollença town trail
From Calvary to Rome

Grade: easy

Distance: 4km

Time: 2 hours

Start & Finish: Via Pollentia, between the Ma-2200 and the town centre

How to get there: There are regular bus services from Port de Pollença to the town. If driving from Lluc, on the Ma-10, take the second exit, heading south, onto the Ma-2200; from the Palma direction, head north towards Pollença on the Ma-2200. In either case, take the Pollença exit opposite a curvy modern monument, almost opposite a car dealership.

Map: a streetmap is available from local shops

Checklist: camera; comfortable shoes; money

Notes: do not be tempted by the "Centro" signs on the Lluc/Port de Pollença road – they only lead you through interminable back streets of no great attraction.

You can easily see the main attractions of this pleasant town in a couple of hours because the historic centre is remarkably compact, yet packed with things to see. Just as Sóller is at the centre for mountain walkers, the old town of Pollença also merits your attention. In common with Sóller, the town was built inland from the port to provide additional defence against the frequent raids of pirates and other would-be invaders.

The Walk

Start from the south end of Via Pollentia (you can usually park in the square between here and the Ma-2200).

1. Walk along the Via Pollentia towards the town centre.

   The tourist information office is located in Carrer Guillem Cifre de Colonya, a couple of blocks to the left from the end of Via Pollentia. Summer: Mon-Fri 08:00 to 16:00 Sat 9:00 to 13:00; Winter: Mon-Fri 08:00 to 15:00 Sun 10:00 to 13:00. Open all year.

2. Continue to the main square – the Plaça Major – dominated by the parish church, opposite, and the charming old Hotel Juma, with its tempting tables, on your right.

   The church of Nostra Senyora dels Angels was founded by the Knights Templar in the 14th century. The 18th-century bell tower was renovated in 1991 to mark the bicentenary of its construction. Inside the church there are paintings depicting the Stations of the Cross

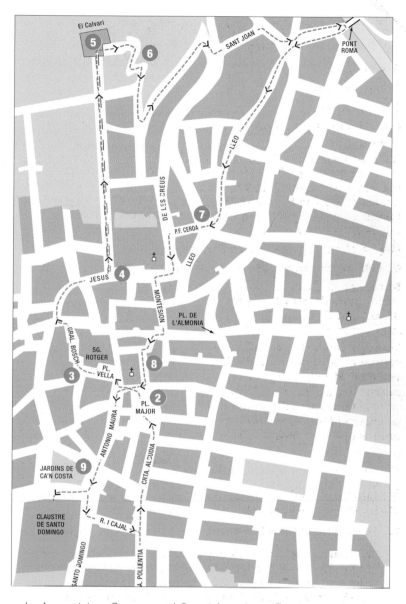

by Argentinian, German and Spanish artists. The sacristy has a collection of icons, paintings and cultural items.

There's an excellent market in the square on Sunday mornings. In mid-January, the Fiesta of St Anthony is celebrated with a bonfire in the centre of the square. Palma has the biggest celebrations, but most towns have their own festivities.

Turn left, in front of the church, into Plaça Vella, then along Carrer de Canonge Rotger.

3. Turn right up Carrer de General Bosch then take a left, to face the elegantly arched property at number 12. Now, turn right along Carrer de Jesús, with its many fine old houses.

4. You'll see the Town Hall (Casa Consistorial) ahead, but leave that until later and turn left up Pollença's biggest attraction – the steps of Carrer del Calvari that lead to the Calvary Chapel.

   There are said to be 365 steps – one for each day of the year and enough (so they say) to discount 12 months of sin – but my wife andd I make it 412. It depends on where you start counting, as there is an initial flight of 48, but that's still not right! Whatever the number, it's an impressive sight and is used for the devallament *(descent from the cross) procession on Good Friday.*

   Part way up, on the right-hand side, be sure to visit the Museum Marti Vicenç. This intriguing collection is based in a 300-year-old house. Marti Vicenç was a craftsman and artist who specialised in textile designs, though he was also a prolific painter and sculptor. The museum, originally a factory shop, features many examples of his work, together with many Mallorcan artefacts – with an emphasis on weaving. If you have visited the town museum in Sóller, you will see several similar rustic items, including wicker products.

5. Continue to the top of the steps and the chapel. Go to the right for a spectacular view of the coast and of the Puig de Santuari. Go back to the chapel and then to the left to "Mirador Vell" – the "old viewpoint" – with views over to the village of Lluc and towards Puig Mayor, the highest mountain on Mallorca.

6. Return down a tarmac road. At a T-junction, go right and then immediately left down the steps. Turn right on Carrer de Sant Joan, do a left/right wiggle to Carrer de Pont Roma – and there's the Roman bridge, constructed over the Torrent de Sant Jordi (St George's Torrent or stream).

   The Pont Roma is almost certainly a 4th-century remnant of Roman rule, though it was possibly *built – almost a heresy to say so – by the Moors a few centuries later. The river bed is invariably dry, but an old photograph from 1898 that I have seen shows plenty of water: a possible indication of how the water supply has been endangered by over-enthusiastic development.*

   Retrace your steps to the junction (marked with a stone cross) and go straight ahead along Carrer del Lleó. Note the stone tethering ring at number 55.

7. Turn right at Carrer de P. Felip Cerdà, left at Carrer de les Creus and then right to the hidden-away church of Esglesia de

Stairway to Calvary

Monti-Sion; this is next to the Casa Consistorial – the Pollença town hall, which was built in 1882. Continue down Carrer de Monti-Sion and then, in the Plaça de Almonia, go right along a paved street, noting the fountain surmounted by a cock – this is the 'Font del Gall', the emblem of Pollença.

8. Continue to the left and you are back in the Plaça Major. Walk across the front entrance to the church and then go left down Carrer de Antonia Maura.

A plaque at number 44 celebrates the life of Miquel Rotger, a local musician – a nice connection with the thriving present-day artistic and cultural life of Pollença.

9. Have a stroll in the attractive gardens of Ca'n Costa. Just across from the gardens, you can also visit the Pollença museum, housed in the 15th-century Dominican convent.

A very reasonable admission charge gets you around the cloisters, chapels and various exhibition rooms. The cloister is the venue for the Pollença Summer Music Festival.

Retrace your steps from the museum and turn right into Carrer de Santo Domingo.

Just before you turn right, pause to inspect the intriguing modern sculpture with the names of famous artists on the spines of books, constructed from bricks.

Choose any left turn to return you to Via Pollentia.

Other places of interest

As a change from Port de Pollença, the nearby coastal resort of **Cala de Sant Vicenç** is worth a visit. See Walk 9 for an easy stroll from here to Port de Pollença. A little further away, **Cap de Formentor** is the northernmost peninsula of Mallorca with its lighthouse perched on a rocky promontory 260 metres above the sea. On a clear day, you can see Menorca, some 40km away. The luxurious **Hotel Formentor** is a virtually self-contained community and its 2000 hectares of grounds include some historically important 13th-century 'casas velles' (old houses).

Other walks in the area

Puig de Maria with its 14th/15th-century chapel, tower and walls is a popular attraction. It is just outside the town and a brisk walk should take an hour each way. You can drive almost to the top, but that's cheating. From the top (330 metres) there are fine views of Formentor and the entire north-east coast. Basic overnight accommodation is available – best to book in advance, tel: 971 184132 .

8. The Boquer Valley

A half-day stroll from Port de Pollença

Grade: easy – but with an optional strenuous side trip

Distance: 8km

Time: 2hrs

Start & Finish: roundabout at the yacht marina, Port de Pollença

How to get there: drive to the seafront and park near the marina. There is a large public car park. There are plenty of buses from other parts of the island.

Map: IGN 644/II & 644/IV (1:25,000 – see reference chart in introduction)

Checklist: walking boots; water; picnic; camera; swimming costume (perhaps); binoculars (see below)

There are surprisingly few walking opportunities in the immediate area of Port de Pollença, and even fewer that are circular, but this one is a classic – even though it's a there-and-back excursion. The Boquer valley is a paradise for birdwatchers. Take your binoculars and a bird-spotting book!

Mountain views from the Coll del Moro in the Boquer valley

The Walk

Start from the yacht marina and walk with the sea on your right (north west). Continue along the pleasant pedestrianised area, passing the hotels Daina and Miramar.

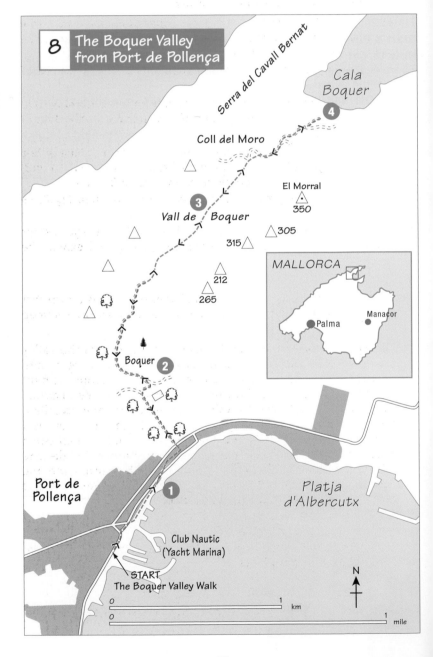

8 The Boquer Valley from Port de Pollença

Serra del Cavall Bernat

Cala Boquer

4

Coll del Moro

El Morral
350

3

Vall de Boquer

305

315

212

265

Boquer

2

MALLORCA

Palma

Manacor

Port de Pollença

Platja d'Albercutx

1

Club Nautic (Yacht Marina)

START
The Boquer Valley Walk

N

0   1
                        km
0   1
                            mile

1. Walk past a small monument and turn left at Avenida Boccharis. Cross a road and walk along a low-walled track through a neglected park area. Cross over the road system to a stony track with a sign to "Predio Boquer" – where almost everything is prohibited, except walking! **(20 mins)**

2. Continue up the track to a set of gates. Go through these to a large house and emerge through a second set of gates. Head to the right, through a third gate, along a wide gravel track.

    Note that a dog was, and still may be, on a long leash – assess its range before you proceed.

    Continue along the obvious track. Climb for a while then cross through a pair of huge rock pillars, after which the entire Boquer valley is revealed.

3. Continue walking, to pass through the Coll del Moro (Pass of The Moor). Go through a wide gap in the stone wall **(50 mins)** and, after just a few minutes, enjoy the view of Cala Boquer.

    Cala Boquer is a delightful spot for a picnic and/or a refreshing dip on a summer's day.

4. Having had your fill of the view, turn back and retrace your steps along the valley. The return is also an hour, going back exactly the same way that you came.

Spicy optional extra:

On the return route, after about 300 metres there is a turn that forks back to the right and into a valley that you may have noticed on the outward route.

To explore this, follow a fairly clear path down into the valley towards a wall and some ruined buildings. You will see a cairn down here – the first of many. Continue uphill, following the most promising path. After a short time you will hit the main cairned route. You do not have to walk far up here for some excellent photo opportunities. If you walk right up to the top there is a fabulous view towards Cala de Sant Vicenç – but an impossible sheer cliff. Other paths do lead off from lower down, but the safe advice is to scramble back down – following the cairns – into the valley. The onward route (which leads to Cala de Sant Vicenç) is far too dangerous for the average walker.

Places of interest

A visit to the town of Pollença is worthwhile – see walk 6, which includes details of other places to visit.

Other walks in the area

Combine this with Walk 9 so that you can visit Cala de Sant Vicenç.

9. Cala de Sant Vicenç to Port de Pollença

From sea to sea – in less than an hour!

Grade: Easy

Distance: 5km

Time: 1 hour

Start & Finish: Cala de Sant Vicenç

How to get there: taxi from Port de Pollença

Map: IGN 644/II (1:25,000 – see reference chart in introduction)

Checklist: Walking boots or strong shoes; water; camera

This short walk can be fitted in as an optional extra before or after the Boquer Valley excursion. Unfortunately, it has to be linear because of possible hazards but, if your party has access to two cars, you can combine the two routes by leaving one car in Cala de Sant Vicenç and the other in Port de Pollença.

Cala de Sant Vicenç from Cala Carbo

The Walk

1. Walk around the seafront of Cala de Sant Vicenç to Cala Carbo – a small cove with fishing boats, but no beach. Look carefully and you will see a sign to Port Pollença.

2. Follow the road, climbing all the time until you reach, literally, the end of the road – with a vehicle turning circle. Head off at about the 11 o'clock position along a track marked by a cairn. Follow the track until (**25 mins**) it ends and continues along a rough path, downhill and slightly to the right. (Another path heads steeply to the right; ignore this – it rejoins the main track later.)

3. Soon, you hit a pleasant path (**40 mins**) and join a track through a pleasant park-like area. Continue to a T-junction (**50 mins**) and turn left. Soon you will come to a main road, where you again turn left and follow your nose into Port de Pollença.

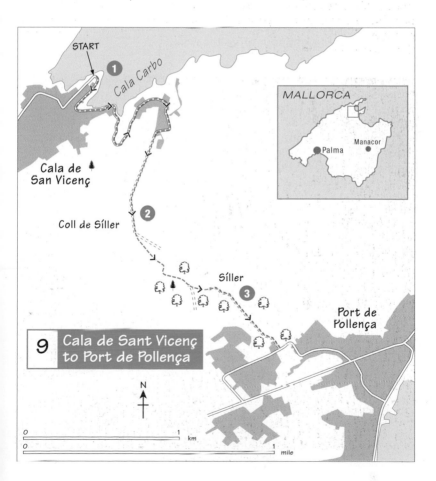

START

Cala Carbo

MALLORCA

Manacor

Palma

Cala de San Vicenç

Coll de Síller

Síller

Port de Pollença

9 Cala de Sant Vicenç to Port de Pollença

N

0   1 km
0   1 mile

10. Alcúdia Peninsula
Platja de S'Illot, La Victoria Hermitage,
Penya des Migdia and the Talaia d'Alcúdia

Grade: easy or moderate or strenuous

Distance: up to 15km

Time: up to 4½ hours

Start & Finish: near the one and only bar at Platja de S'Illot

How to get there: drive from Alcúdia through the Mal Pas and Bon Aire developments. Stay on the northern coast road for about 3.5km, passing a smart marina, until you reach the parking area opposite the bar on the beach of Platja de S'Illot, almost opposite the small island of S'Illot. Or, take a taxi from Alcúdia.

Map: IGN 645/III (1:25,000 – see reference chart in introduction)

Checklist: walking boots; water; picnic; camera

Notes: while you are in the area, be sure to visit the town of Alcúdia – there's a short walking tour after this walk.

The entire walk is in the 1000-hectare La Victoria national park, an area of land owned by Alcúdia Town Council. A huge variety of plants awaits you, including dwarf palms (thousands of them), plus asphodels, cistus and – in the springtime – orchids. There are also some very handsome wild (so-called 'Quality') goats and the occasional donkey for extra photo opportunities!

The Walk

Start by having a coffee at the bar – it's a pleasant place with great views of the coast. Then, leave the bar and walk along the road with the sea on your left.

1. Turn right at a tarmac lane marked as a No Through Road and with several other signs. After just a few metres, turn left into a hollow between two large concrete blocks then right – uphill – through the woods and initially parallel to the road on a wide stony track, marked with blue arrows.

    Be sure not to start on the narrower path to the right – this is where you will return at the end of the walk.

2. Fork left from the main track **(15 mins)** with a sign pointing to Ermita de la Victoria and Talaia d'Alcúdia.

3. A steepening uphill track eventually leads to the car park of the hermitage **(25 mins)**.

    A 5-minute break is allowed for here. There are toilets – and water to replenish your supplies. There is also a bar/restaurant for the weary

S'Illot from the bar at the start of the walk

– and the very weary can cut the walk short by heading down the road from the car park to the coast and back to the start.

Continue on the old forestry track which leads uphill, behind the hermitage, and pass a barrier across the road.

4. After a sharp right-hand bend (**45mins**), there are steps with a wooden handrail ahead and to your left, which is the start of an optional extra excursion taking about an hour. If you are NOT doing this, skip to point 6

Side trip: optional excursion to Penya des Migdia

This will add an extra hour (approx.) to your walk:

Go left up the steps with handrail alongside. Continue around the hillside to an open area (**15mins**) from where you can make a there-and-back ascent of the 387-metre peak of Puig des Romani, for some fabulous views.

5. Otherwise, continue for a further five minutes, passing a small stone construction, to the old lookout tower at the end of Penya des Migdia (**25mins**). Squeeze through the small entrance and out the other side for an excellent view of the Bay of Pollença.

If you fancy a further exploration, follow the steep path to the right and you will find an old cannon, part of the old fortifications. Otherwise, retrace your steps to point 4 on the main track (**55mins**). From here, turn left and go uphill along the wide forestry track.

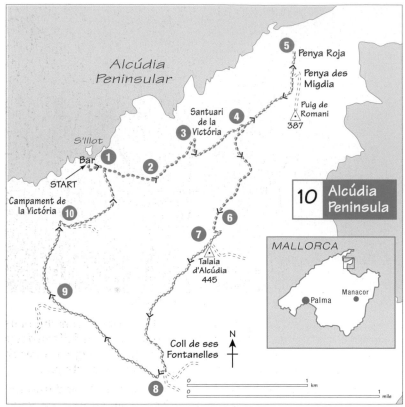

End of optional excursion: main walk continues here

6. The forestry track levels out at an open area before the final assault on the Talaia d'Alcudia. Passing the foot of the mountain **(1hr)** you approach a wire fence. Turn left at the signpost and follow the waymarks, passing a three-way signpost **(1hr 15mins)** before the trig point at the top, where there are a couple of stone buildings and a forest fire look-out station **(1hr 20mins)**.

Have a well-earned break 10-minute break here!

7. From the top, most people retrace their steps for about 150 metres and then turn right to Coll Baix. This is tedious; a far more scenic alternative is the less well-used route that heads south-west along a ridge, as follows:

Face south-west from the peak, with sea to both left and right. Set off along the ridge and keep to the right – *this is the only safe route*. Scramble down a short way to the right and you are soon off the steep part and safely on the ridge, where the path is clear.

Keep on the crest of the ridge for the next half-hour, following occasional cairns – and very occasional faded red paint dots – as

Wild goats below Talaia d'Alcudia

the path continues roughly south-west. Do not stray from this path or head off to left or right. Your destination is the head of the deep valley coming in from the right, so there is quite a long way to walk – but you will always find an occasional cairn to guide you.

Eventually the path heads a little more to the south and towards the head of the valley. Soon, you arrive at a junction – and some welcome shade – at the pass of Coll de ses Fontanelles **(2hrs 5mins)** with a sign to "Ermita de la Victoria 1hr 30mins".

This is an excellent place for lunch, so 15 minutes is allowed for here.

8. Cross the pass on a track, i.e. following the *ermita* sign, and turn right. Head down the side of the ravine to join the path alongside the *torrent* **(2hrs 25mins)**. The path crosses and re-crosses the torrent before climbing to a wider track – still in the same direction as the *torrent* and is still waymarked to the *ermita*. You must ignore all side tracks, even those with blue arrows!

9. After a few more minutes, the track swings to the right **(2hrs 45mins)** over the hillside to give you some gorgeous views – of the Talaia d'Alcúdia to the right and, in springtime, flowers all around you. There is a small housing development over to the left.

10. At a junction **(2hrs 55mins)**, there is a signpost pointing left to Campanet and right to the Ermita. Turn right here for just 70 metres, then left at a blue arrow – ignoring the waymark post pointing straight ahead. Walk along this blue-arrowed track, ignoring all side turns as you first move away from the sea then

swing back on course. Soon, you reach the ravine where we started the walk, albeit on the other side of the torrent. Turn left and you are back at your starting point (**3hrs 10mins**).

Places of interest

Alcúdia is surrounded by areas of interest to naturalists. In addition to La Victoria, **Albufereta**, to the west of the city, has 150 hectares of dunes and wetlands. The peninsula of **Cap des Pinar** is a 2500-hectare site noted for its variety of plants and birdlife. South of Port d'Alcúdia is the wetland nature reserve of **S'Albufera** – a 2200-hectare national park of great interest to birdwatchers. A free visitor permit can be obtained at the reception centre.

The remains of the Roman city of **Pollentia** are just south of Alcúdia. Quintus Metellus, the general who led the Roman invasion of Mallorca, founded it in 122BC. The Roman theatre, able to seat up to 2000 people, was built in the first century AD and is still used for concerts and similar events. The Pollentia site was excavated by the Bryant Foundation (see below) from 1957 to 1997. For much fuller information, go to this web site:

www.dartmouth.edu/~classics/oldsite/PollentiaNet/PollentiaNet.html

Other walks in the area

The helpful tourist office in Port d'Alcúdia has a collection of (free) walks leaflets. There is also a leaflet of cycle tours – this includes a route equally suitable for walkers from Alcúdia around the various Roman remains to the south of the town.

Alcúdia town mini-trail

One "walk" that should not be missed is a stroll around the historic centre of Alcúdia. You hardly need a map, but you can get one as a souvenir from local shops.

Alcúdia is the oldest city on Mallorca, dating from Phoenician times. The Romans were the next to appear, establishing the settlement of Pollentia near to the present-day city in 123 BC. The name Alcúdia first appeared during Moorish occupation, though there appear to be no visible remains of this period. After the invasion of Jaime I in 1229, Alcúdia and its port became important components of the newly expanded empire. From the 14th century, the city was surrounded by rings of defensive walls, which have been partially restored.

There is not as much to see as in Pollença or Sóller, but enough to while away an hour or so. Park on the south side of town, in the market area, Passeig de Pere Ventayol, just off the Avengida dels Princeps d'Espanya. Walk north to Plaça de Carles V and then along the busy Carrer del Moll to the main square, Plaça de la Constitució.

Walk through the square to pass the Ajuntament (town hall) on your left. This impressive civic building, with its clock and bell tower, was completed in 1929.

From here, make a there-and-back visit to view the house on your right-hand side called Ca'n Carta with its ornate mullioned windows. Now continue on your main route. Go through the small square – Placeta des les Verdoles – and walk along Carrer dels Albellons, passing the building of the Bryant Hispano-America Archaeological Foundation. William J. Bryant bought the site of the Pollentia Roman

The attractive town hall of Alcúdia

theatre in 1952 and, a year later, bought this house from which to direct his excavations.

Turn right at Carrer de Sant Jaume and you reach the Parish church of St James (Sant Jaume) – a 19th-century building set in an attractive open area just inside the old city wall. Outside the church, there are interesting multi-lingual accounts of the history of Mallorca.

11. Petra and the Ermita de Bonany
Californian connections

Grade: Moderate

Distance: 7km

Time: 1hr to 2½hrs

Start & Finish: The Juniper Serra Museum – clearly signposted in Petra.

How to get there: Petra lies between Inca and Manacor. Arriving in the small town, follow signs for the museum then park in the public car park in Carrer de la Victoria Vella. From the car park, walk down Carrer des Barracar Alt to the museum.

Map: IGN 699/II (1:25,000 – see reference chart in introduction)

Checklist: Walking boots; water; picnic; camera; money

The small town of Petra is about 12km north-west of Manacor. Being in the central "Pla" region, the town is away from the tourism zones and local people are now trying to re-establish agriculture on a larger and more profitable scale. Viniculture is being developed, though cereals are the main crop at present. The church, (Ermita de Bonany) was built in 1609. The name "Bonany" means "good year" and recalls a time when, after a prolonged drought in 1609, the prayers of the villagers for rain were miraculously answered; basic accommodation available – advance bookings recommended; tel: 971-826568).

The village's main claim to fame is that Miguel Serra y Aloran, later to be known as Father Juniper Serra, was born here on 24th November 1713. He became a preacher, but was so small that he could scarcely see over the lectern when delivering his sermons. At the age of 36, he decided to be a missionary and was sent by his church to present-day Mexico. After 18 years of missionary work there, he moved on to what is now San Diego in California. The Father Serra Chapel, built in 1776 in San Juan de Capistrano commemorates his name; this is said to be the oldest building in California. He died on 28th August 1784. (It is even claimed that California was discovered by him and that its name is a corruption of the Mallorquin for hot (cali) and oven (forn) ... a possibility, but no more than that!)

The museum in the village (donation requested) is interesting for a short visit though I felt a bit uneasy to see the paintings that depicted the conversion of the North American Indians to Christianity, with some considerable loss of their own culture. Visit and decide for yourself.

The Walks

From the museum, walk uphill, passing Juniper Serra's birthplace just a few metres later, on the same side of the street as the museum. The

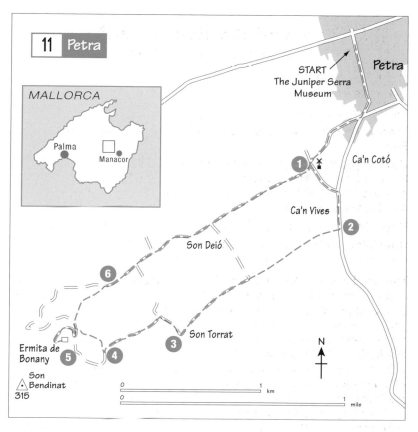

street has recently been pedestrianised and is now very attractive with tubs of plants along the way. At the top of this street, turn right along Rectoria Vella then left at a T-junction and choose from either:

A there-and-back walk:

1. Continue straight ahead, towards the Ermita, **keeping right** at the circular base of an old windmill. After approximately 30mins, fork left at a tarmac lane signed as Camí Vell de Bonany then, after climbing a short way, fork right at a bollarded but unsigned uphill concrete path, Where this hits the road, turn left then right at the next bollarded track and continue upwards in a similar fashion, with the tracks simply cutting out the loops in the road.

    Soon, the steps to the Ermita de Bonany are ahead. Climb these and you arrive at the entrance. After visiting the church, skip to point 5 on page 63 and retrace your steps to Petra.

    You can, of course, have a shorter walk by parking (with consideration) at an intermediate point along the road. You could even drive all the way up to the Ermita, and scarcely walk at all!

The Ermita de Bonany

A longer, circular walk:

1. Begin by heading towards the Ermita, but this time **keep left** at the circular base of the old windmill, and head towards the Ma-3310 Manacor road.

2. Walk along the main road, away from Petra, then – 100 metres past a large storage depot on the right-hand side – turn right down the *very first lane on the right* after the depot **(15 mins)**. You can be sure that this really *is* the correct lane as, although it is unsigned, there is a yellow waymark on the stones near the start of the lane and a 'Stop' sign where it meets the main road. *(Do **not** take the second lane to the right, Camí de Sa Cova).*

    Continue along this lane, with the Ermita de Bonany ahead, on the Puig de Maria, and some attractive properties to admire, until you reach the end of the tarmac **(45 mins)**.

    According to local tradition, "Puig de Maria" derived its name from the hiding of a statue of the Virgin Mary during the Moorish occupation. A lot of this went on in Mallorca.

3. Almost exactly at the end of the tarmac, turn right through a rustic gate ('rustic' = a few sticks wired together and a wire loop as a catch) with, in 2008, a very faint yellow waymark dot that may be all but invisible by the time you read this. Continue along a wide track – taking care not to veer left into a farmyard. Intermittent yellow dots and arrows mark the route.

There has been a report of a gate being placed between points (3) and (4) on the waymarked route; this may, by now, have been removed but walkers have been able to circumvent the problem by climbing over the wall or taking a slightly longer route.

4. Follow the track until it levels out and then take a sharp hairpin to the right, uphill, along a narrower track **(1hr 5mins)**. This eventually **(1hr 10mins)** crosses a tarmac road, twice.

    Soon, the steps to the Ermita de Bonany are ahead. Climb these and you arrive at the entrance **(1hr 15mins)**.

    In addition to the church, there's a vending machine and a shop that sells tourist souvenirs. On a clear day there are excellent views from the terrace.

5. After a 15-minute break it's time to return to Petra. Leave the car park and go back down the steps. At the tarmac road be sure to turn *left*, so that you get to Petra by the shortest route. Go downhill on tarmac then right down a bollarded concrete track. This again hits the road, where you turn left, then down the next track on the right – and so on, all the way down.

6. Emerge on a tarmac lane and continue down to the more major (but quiet) road leading to Petra.

    This is the reverse of the there-and-back route.

    Follow the road for 2km all the way back to the town, ignoring a left turn into Camí de Son Homar. After passing the old windmill, fork left along Carrer des Barracar Baix then take the second right into Carrer de la Rectoria Vella, back to the car park **(2hrs 15mins for the circular walk)**.

Other Walks in the area

Few in the immediate vicinity, but Santa Eugenia and Algaida are only a short drive away. See walks 15, 16 and 17.

Places of interest

The **Torrent de Na Borges**, a few kilometres to the north-east, is a naturalists' paradise. For details, see leaflet available from the town hall. **Montuiri** and **Manacor**, both famous for their pearl factories, are each a 15-minute drive away – see notes at the end of the Algaida and Randa walk (Walk 15). The old manor house and estate of **Els Calderers** is a similar distance away – see www.elscalderers.com.

12. Cap de Ferrutx
Mallorca's most beautiful coastline?

Grade: easy/moderate – just a few short ascents

Distance: 9km

Time: 3½ hrs

Start & Finish: Cala Estreta (or Cala Mesquida, see below)

How to get there: drive from Arta in the direction of Cala Rajada and, after leaving the town, turn left after a petrol station at the sign to "Cala Torta". Pass the fire station, then the football ground and continue towards the sea. After about 7km, pass between a pair of gateposts, keeping to the left and ignoring the sign to Cala Torta. Just beyond the gateposts, stop the car because, since the first edition of this book, the road has deteriorated very significantly. You have two options:

Normal car: continue for a short distance and park at the open area before the road starts to descend, otherwise there is a very good chance that you will damage your car. Having parked, walk the remaining kilometre or so, keeping left along the potholed road.

Very robust 4x4: you may be able to drive down to the original start point at Cala Estreta, and park looking out to sea, but you'll need a tough vehicle to do it.

Alternatively: start the walk from Cala Mesquida, about 2km along the coast from Cala Torta. Take a taxi to Cala Mesquida from Cala Rajada – the nearest large resort.

Map: IGN 672/II (1:25,000 – see reference chart in introduction)

Checklist: walking boots; water; picnic; camera; swimming costume (possibly!)

Notes: though this is a fairly easy walk, it is very exposed and there is absolutely no shelter from the sun on the return journey. Take **plenty** of water.

The beaches along this stretch of coast are idyllic – especially the one at the very end of the walk, just below S'Arenalet. Don't be over-confident of being completely alone, as we once blundered onto the beach at entirely the wrong time (though one of my readers was most disappointed not to have had the same experience!).

It seems odd to find this small network of roads – with no development and only the occasional beach bar. I can only assume that it was the work of speculators many years ago and that the area has been abandoned, at least for the time being. It's worth the visit for, as the same reader commented: "Really weird rocky stretch back along the coast – bit like Lanzarote. A terrific walk and well worth the hairy car ride to the starting point".

The Walk

By one means or another, you should be at the tiny bay of Cala Estreta. There is now a problem to consider: in order to make the walk circular, the outward route that I describe entails a minor trespass – one that walkers have been guilty of for many years. If you do not wish to follow in their footsteps, make your own way along the coastal path (see sketch map) to the beach at S'Arenalet and return from point 6. If you prefer to do the complete, circular walk, follow these instructions:

1. Walk back up the potholed road, in the reverse direction to the way you arrived. Just 50 metres past a white metal post, where a prominent track crosses the road, turn right **(7 mins)**. After 30 metres turn right again to a wall surmounted by a wire fence where you turn right again. Follow the wall for a few metres and you will see a well-trodden gap in the fence – go through here.

   This gap has been used for several years. There is another fence that you will encounter later with a similar gap, and they both enclose this unused land. But there is nothing to enclose, no stock to wander, no property to damage, so what is the landowner protecting? If the gaps are closed permanently, this walk will just have to be a simple coastal one, but that would detract considerably from the enjoyment.

   Having gone through the gap, turn left towards a pair of high locked gates, go ahead (as if you had passed through the gates) and fork right. Then continue straight ahead, ignoring all paths to the left.

2. Enter some woods **(20 mins)** and turn left (cairn) along a wide track.

   You can now see the prominent Torre d'Albarca – an old look-out tower that we visit on the return section of this trip.

   Still heading towards the tower, follow the wiggling path down towards Cala Matzoc. As the path levels, keep left – away from, but parallel to, the coast – and descend through pines to the top end of the beach **(35 mins)**.

3. Cross the sandy beach to a track. Go to the right and then, after 50 metres, head left – soon heading north-west through a clearing and gently uphill. The path levels out at a fork **(45 mins)**. Turn left (south-west) here to follow a path that curves around a small bay below and to the left. Be sure to stay on the wide, stony track along the top of the ridge until you come to a fence **(55 mins)**. This is the fence that we mentioned at the start of the walk – it runs parallel to the first one that you went through.

4. Go through a large gap to the left of the gate.

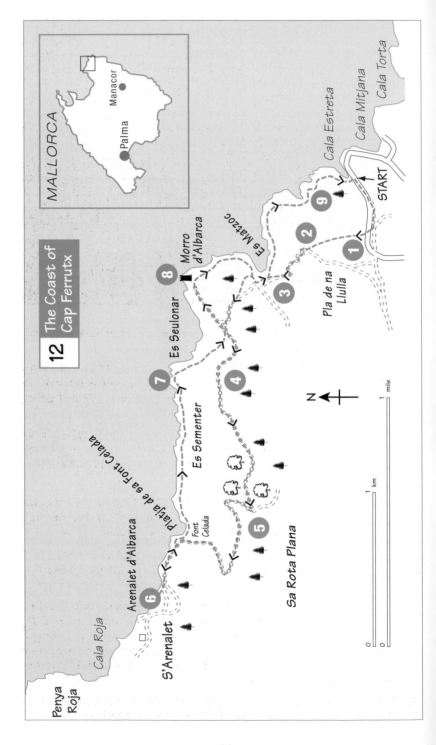

Torre d'Albarca

If the fence becomes impassable here, follow the fence seawards and use the coastal path instead.

Continue with the conical shape of Puig de Sa Font ahead. Soon **(1hr 5mins)** keep right at the fork and you will see antennae on the skyline as a marker (but *only* as a marker – we're not going there!)

5. A few minutes after the fork, turn right at a T-junction. The hill on the skyline, topped with a tower, is Talaia de Moreia. The track winds downhill to the left of Platja de sa Font Celada (= beach of the salty, or brackish, spring).

6. Continue along the coast to the beach at S'Arenalet (S'Arenalet des Verger). Although our walk returns from here, the main track continues for those who wish to investigate further.

    The perfection is marred only by winter debris swept off the sea. Perhaps we should all take some of the rubbish back to the nearest waste bins.

7. Return along the coast and cross Platja de Sa Font Celada, but this time *on the seaward side* to a path opposite. Keep to the coastal path – obvious but often rough underfoot. Continue along a mainly volcanic surface of ever-changing colours. The flat rock reflects the summer sun to an intense degree – it feels like the surface of an alien planet.

8. Eventually you catch sight again of the Torre d'Albarca and go through a gap at the bottom of a fence **(2hrs 25mins)**.

This is a continuation of the same (second) fence that we encountered on our outward journey. Since the gap is (I hope!) always open, any goats or sheep can wander at will, so why have a fence?

From here, climb steeply up to the trees. Then follow a winding, woodland path in a generally seaward direction until you reach the tower **(2hrs 35mins)**.

9. You may still be able to go into the tower and – with care – climb the stairs to look out of the windows. Admire the craftsmanship – the stones in the arches fit as closely as if they had been cut by a modern-day machine – but this was constructed in the 16th century.

From the tower, continue along the cliff-top path and cross the beach of Es Matzoc. Follow the cairned path over the headland (away from the sea) and you reach a gate (always open) at the foot of a fence – the other end of the first fence we met on our walk!

Go through the gateway **(3hrs)**; keep right to avoid a landslip and continue along this delightful coastal path to arrive at the rocky inlet of Cala Estreta **(3hrs 15mins)** and your car – unless you started at Cala Mesquida, of course.

Time for a cooling drink. Make your way to Cala Mitjana and hope that the beach bar is open. Or try the next bay of Cala Torta (partly nudist).

Other walks in the area

Not very many, though you can take a bus or taxi from Cala Rajada to Capdepera, visit the castle and walk back. There is also a pleasant stroll from the centre of Cala Rajada to the lighthouse.

Places of interest

Cala Rajada – alternative spelling Cala Ratjada – is mainly a resort town, but it has a pleasant harbour and a market on Saturday; the March banking foundation has an interesting modern sculpture park just outside the town centre. **Capdepera**, 2km south-west of Cala Rajada has a castle. **Artà** is the principal town in the area with a splendid hilltop fortress and the Sanctuary of St. Salvador. Historic Artà has been occupied for over 3000 years, as evidenced by the Bronze Age site at Ses Paisses on the edge of town – see website: www.idealspain.com/pages/Places/mallorca/sespaisses.htm

The distant Tramuntana range from near to Castellitx (Walk 16)

Central & Southern

13. Castell d'Alaró
A castle, a chapel and a restaurant

Grade: moderate

Distance: 7km

Time: approx 2hrs

Start & Finish: **either** the roadside near the 12km marker on the Ma-2100 from Orient to Alaró **or** the car park near the Es Verger restaurant on the access road from Alaró to the castle.

How to get there:

Option 1, for which car parking is a bit of a gamble: from either Bunyola through Orient or from Alaró in the direction of Orient; the precise starting point is about 100km from the 12km marker post in the direction of Orient. There are a few parking places towards Alaró. In desperation, there is a car park in the village of Orient.

For the second option, it is best to start from Alaró in the direction of Orient on the Ma-2100 and, after 1km, turn left at the sign for Es Verger and Castell d'Alaró. It is then a 4km uphill, very winding, narrow road to the car park.

Map: IGN 670/IV (1:25,000 – see reference chart in introduction)

Checklist: walking boots; water; picnic; camera; money

Notes: Two walks, of similar lengths, are described: either a simple there-and-back from the 12km marker on the Ma-2100 from Orient to Alaró or a circular from the car park near the Es Verger restaurant.

In the first edition of this book I described an alternative return route back to the 12km marker via Ca'n Sollerich. I decided against it this time as there is an unavoidable 2km walk along the Ma-2100. Today's increased traffic makes this too dangerous, but drop me a line via the publisher and I will be pleased to send a copy of the directions from the first edition.

Option 1 – from the 12km marker to the car park

From the marker, walk towards Orient for about 100 metres to a gateway and a wooden sign to "Castell", this being the start of the walk.

1. Walk past a water storage tank on your left and stay on the main track, ignoring any turnings. After **15mins** walk through a wooded area and pass a circular clearing, possibly the site of a *sitja*, where wood from the forest was burnt for charcoal.

2. After **25 mins**, pause to enjoy a wonderful view of the Orient Valley. Soon, you reach the car park used by those who chose Option 2, so go left here and continue with the following instructions that apply to Option 2.

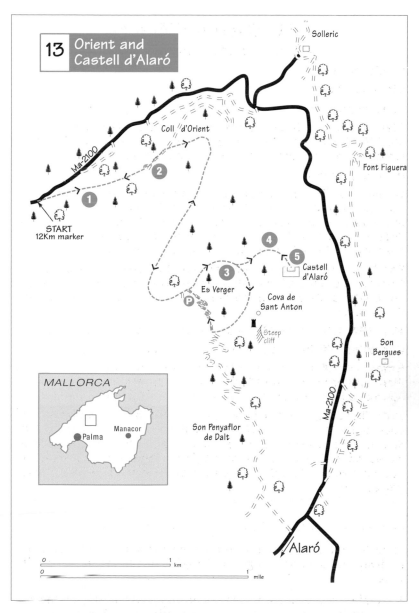

Option 2: Drive to the car park

If you decide against driving up to Es Verger you can, of course, walk there but it's quite a slog and there's not much to describe, except to say that you can cut out some of the zig-zags (look for the red blobs!). What you cannot do is to drive part-way up, because there are absolutely no parking spaces from the bottom to the top!

Presuming that you have walked either from the 12km marker or driven all the way from Alaro to Es Verger and parked your car (*not* in the restaurant car park if not using the facilities) and recovered from the 4km drive up the mountain, this is what you now do:

> Walk out of the car park, and follow the main route uphill. After about **15mins** you will see a sign telling you that there's 15mins still to go to reach the top – this is very optimistic for the average walker, so don't despair.

3. Eventually **(40 mins/1hr 5mins),** you arrive at a sign to Castell (left) or Alaró (right).

   If you do not go to the Castell you will miss all the views, the chapel, a dose of history and the reward of a coffee (or beer etc). There's no question – onwards and upwards to the castle!

4. Climb the stepped path and pass through the first of two archways **(45 mins/1hr 10mins)** into the outer grounds of the castle. Follow the path generally uphill and bear left to admire the view then follow the main track to the highest point. Just below the summit **(50 mins/1hr 15mins)** look right towards Alaró and, closer to, the Es Verger restaurant.

5. Arrive at the top **(1 hour/1hour 25mins)** and be sure to visit the chapel before heading for the bar.

   The castle is strategically well placed to withstand a siege – as it did in 1285 during one of Mallorca's many wars, this time between Alfonso III of Aragón and Jaime III, grandson of Jaime I, The

The entrance to the grounds of Castell d'Alaró

Conquistador. Guillen Cabrit and Guillen Bassa nobly resisted the siege of Alaró but starvation forced them to surrender, after which they were roasted alive by Alfonsó's men. Paintings of Cabrit and Bassa hang in the chapel, together with a framed article (in the small room on the right) about their heroism. They are unofficially regarded as saints – though Mallorca has only one 'proper' saint, Catalina Thomàs.

I included a visit from the castle to the Cova de Sant Anton (St Anthony's Cave) in the first edition. At the time of this revision (2008), this was not possible due to extensive restoration and development works in the main castle complex. In this edition the excursion to the cave has been omitted as I suspect that the works will take a long time to complete. Perhaps a reader will keep me informed.

Back to the start

Having visited the castle, stop the clock and re-start timings for the descent. Return to the three-way signpost (**10mins** – point 3 on map). And then, **For those who have walked from the 12km marker**, it is best to take the direct route to the car park by following the Alaró/Es Pouet sign and simply retrace the outward route to the car – about 40 minutes.

For those who started in the car park, here is a slightly longer route to make the walk circular: from the three-way signpost, take the route that simply says "Alaró"– i.e. the one to the left as you come down from the castle. Walk down the rough track that soon becomes better surfaced and runs alongside a recently restored stone wall.

After 20 minutes you hit a waymark post. Be sure to take a hairpin to the right here, then continue for a few minutes until you reach a road – this being the one that climbs from near to Alaró. Turn right here, and walk uphill for 10 minutes to the car park.

If you have not parked your car near the Es Verger, turn left where you reach the road and walk down this to wherever you started.

Other walks in the area

A lengthy linear route (14km) links Santa Maria and Orient – see "Landscapes of Mallorca" by Valeri Crespi-Green for details. An interesting route in the Orient/Bunyola area is described in www.mallorcafact.com/slideshow/orient/orientwalk.htm.

Places of interest

Orient is the nearest small town – it lies about 2km west from one of the start-points of the walk. The famous L'Hermitage hotel is even nearer – but a change of clothing may be a good idea! Heading south-west for a further 5km of winding roads, you reach the large town of **Bunyola** with its photogenic station and – out of season – hundreds of cyclists on their way to or from the Orient valley.

14. Mancor de la Vall
The Hermitage of Santa Llúcia

Grade: Moderate

Distance: 2km or 4km

Time: Between one and two hours

Start & Finish: the town hall, in the centre of Mancor

How to get there: Inca is the nearest large town. Drive from here towards Lloseta; the village of Mancor is 3km north of Lloseta.

Map: IGN 671/III (1:25,000 – see reference chart in introduction)

Checklist: Walking boots; water; picnic; camera; money

Mancor de la Vall is an attractive small village founded in 1232. The hermitage dedicated to Santa Llúcia (patron saint for sufferers of eye diseases) is a large building – more like a large hotel – at the top of the prominent hill just outside the village. A tarmac road leads all the way up to the hermitage, but a mainly off-road route is described – with an alternative return route

The parish church in Mancor de la Vall

The Walk

The main square, with the town hall (look for the flags) and the large parish church, is a pleasant place to start – perhaps after a visit to the Bar Ca's Puput (Mallorquin for Hoopoe). Start the walk by passing the entrance to the church, ignoring the road signs to Santa Llucia.

1. Continue uphill and take the second left along Carrer de Sa Costa. At a T-junction, go right – still uphill. A tarmac lane swings right then left past some houses to be greeted by a ceramic plaque marking the third Station of the Cross. This is the start of today's pilgrimage!

    Turn right along an upward-sloping track, and soon you are walking up some steps.

    In 2008 some flimsy metal-bar barriers were in place to prevent a horse from escaping. No problem for humans, though.

2. Cross a road **(15 mins)**, continue up more steps, and the occasional station of the cross, to where you meet the road again. Turn left and continue to the top **(25 mins)**. Use any convenient short cuts along the way to eliminate parts of the zig-zagging tarmac.

    There's a small chapel (usually closed) but the hermitage may be open. If so, step inside to admire the courtyard. Outside, there are wonderful view to Inca, with its nearby mountain of Santa Magdalena, and across to the Bay of Alcúdia.

3. After a 10-minute breather, you can go back the way you came – total time about 1¼ hours including the break at the top.

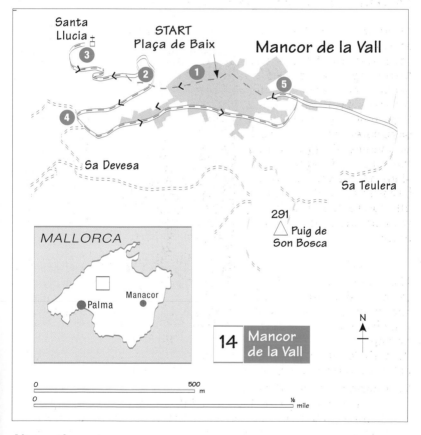

Alternative return

Here's an alternative return route that lengthens the walk:

> At the bottom of the first set of steps (where you can cross a road to a house to return by the direct route) turn right and stay on the tarmac road.

4. After five minutes, the road sweeps to the left. Half-way round the bend, after crossing a river bed, there is a small building decorated with agricultural implements.

In the previous edition of this book, I described a 4km route that turned right at this point and zig-zagged uphill for 25 minutes, then swung left along a downhill track across Sa Devesa to Sa Teulera and back to the start. Unfortunately, this cannot now be completed because of housing developments and closures of paths. If you find an alternative in this area, let me know.

After investigating just about every tempting path around Mancor, and speaking to the not-very-helpful town hall staff, here is a much less adventurous alternative ending:

Walk past the implement-decorated house, heading back towards Mancor, then go past a neo-classical columned building.

5. Approaching the fountain at a crossroads, turn right. Pass Villa la Conchita – a fine building (one-time

The Moorish wash-house

hotel?) of faded elegance. After this, visit the restored Moorish water supply and wash-house before returning to the town centre.

Other walks in the area

A walk from Mancor, along Cami de la Font Garrover, is described in www.allaboutmallorca.com/Olive-Grove-Walks.html. There is also a pleasant short walk to Puig d'Inca, 5km east of Inca, giving excellent views.

Places to visit

Lloseta is about 3km to the south. Once famed for its leather crafts, from the beginning of the 20th century it became a centre for coal mining. The last pit closed in 1973. Just outside the town centre, the gardens of the Aiamans Palace are open to the public on Saturday and Sunday afternoons. The commercial centre for the area is **Inca**, famed for its market (Thursday, Friday and Sunday). Inca has many interesting buildings, including the 18th/19th-century parish church and two convents from the same periods.

15. Algaida and Randa
Exploring the central plain

Grade: easy/moderate

Distance: 12km

Time: 4 hours

Start & Finish: the main square in the centre of Algaida

How to get there: Algaida is approximately 15km east of Palma, off the Ma-15 road to Manacor. Turn off the main road and head for the church tower. There is a regular bus service, but note that the village lies about a kilometre south of the main road.

Map: IGN 699/III (1:25,000 – see reference chart in introduction)

Checklist: walking boots; water; picnic; camera

Notes: there's an excellent baker and pastrycook near to the café at the top right-hand corner of the square in Algaida.

Algaida may be only 15km from Palma, but it might as well be on the next planet. It's a delightfully sleepy town where life continues at a pleasantly slow pace. There are many interesting features, including the five stone crosses from the 16th to 18th centuries that mark the boundaries of the town, and its 17 windmills – some scarcely recognisable as such. In the centre of the town there is the huge 16th/17th century parish church; one of its many side-chapels contains the tomb of Bartholomé Pou, the Algaida-born biographer of Catalina Thomàs, Mallorca's only saint.

The Walk

Start in Sa Plaça – Algaida's main square. Facing uphill, aim for the top left corner of the square. Go past Café Suc and along Carrer de San Joan.

1. Turn left along Carrer del Migdia and you come to a large cross at a junction. Go right here, then first left along Carrer des Campet **(15 mins)**. Just before a mill, turn left along Carrer de Cubrit i Bassa (these are the names of the two unofficial Mallorcan saints that we met on the Castell d'Alaró walk). Go over a cross-roads and bear right along Carrer de son Miguel Joan; straight ahead, you can see the hill of Puig de Caldent.

2. You soon leave all traces of traffic when you pass a mill **(30 mins)** and fork left along the Camí de Son Roig.

3. Pass Ca'n Manjo **(50 mins)** and, a few minutes later, a large farm, Son Roig, where the road surface starts to deteriorate. Very soon, fork right through woods and the track then swings left at Villa Susanna **(1hr 5mins)**.

Son Roig farmhouse

Moments later, look left to Puig de Cura, with an incongruous dome on its top. This will be a very useful landmark for the rest of the walk.

Go past a ramshackle collection of farm outbuildings, hen sheds and the like. Pass the entrance to Ca'n Rectoria **(1hr 15mins)** on your right and, as you walk along, watch out for a track forking to the right. You don't use this but, just after this minor landmark, start looking to the left through the hedge to spot a concrete blockhouse in the field. Just 50 metres later, look for a pair of gateposts about 200 metres across the field, again to your left.

It is important that you see these – otherwise you are destined for a lengthy walk along a dangerous main road. Do not depend on continuing to the next left turn that is marked on the map near to Son Saleta; although it starts promisingly, it is comprehensively blocked!

4a. About 100 metres after you spotted the gateposts, start looking for a gap on your left. It may still be marked by a small cairn, built by me a few years ago. This is where the track should be, to within a few metres. If you can't find it, go to point 4b, below, instead.

Jump down at this point, cross a wide ditch and keep to the left. Follow the field edge, marked by an overgrown hedge, on your left and walk towards, and between, the gateposts.

4b. If option 4a is no longer viable, try this instead: about 50m before the suggested cairned gap, go through a wide gap on the left and walk along the wall of an old reservoir for a few metres. Then drop

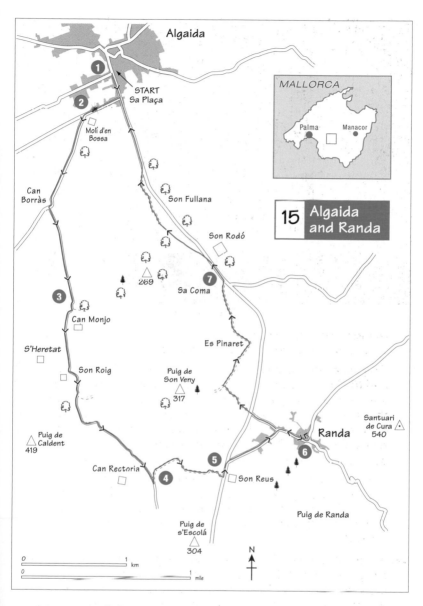

Algaida

START
Sa Plaça

Molí d'en
Bossa

Can
Borràs

Son Fullana

Son Rodó

MALLORCA

Palma   Manacor

15 Algaida
and Randa

269

Sa Coma

Can Monjo

Es Pinaret

S'Heretat

Son Roig

Puig de
Son Veny
317

Santuari
de Cura
540

Puig de
Caldent
419

Can Rectoria

Randa

Son Reus

Puig de Randa

Puig de
s'Escolá
304

N

0   1
          km
0   1
                  mile

down, turn left and follow the field edge until you reach the
gateposts – which are not visible at first.

After the gateposts – however you arrived – keep to the right,
heading straight towards the Cura peak with Randa below. At a
pair of metal gates, turn right along the obvious track (**1hr
25mins**). Pass a cow/sheep-shed on your left then fork left – still
on the main track, and still with Puig de Randa ahead.

5. Go through a gate (close and latch it afterwards) and you join the main road (**1hr 30mins**) with the buildings of Son Reus facing you. Go left here and walk, facing the fast traffic, for a mercifully short 100 metres along the busy main road. Turn right to Randa and then walk almost 1km up the tarmac road to the village centre (**1hr 45mins**).

Note: The timings from here assume a 20-minute break in Randa.

The "just in case" route

If for any reason the route I have described becomes impassable or if you simply miss the turning, you may have to continue all the way to the main road. If so, here are some brief directions, which attempt to reduce the road walking to a minimum:

Continue from point 4 and pass a junction, with the large Son Saleta building on your right and the Puig de S'Escola (304m) on your left. According to the map you should be able to turn left here. However, the track is blocked. Eventually, you reach the main road from Llucmajor. Cross this to a minor road and pass Es Ranxo on your right. Follow the high wire fence on your left as the road bends to the left. The tarmac ends as you come to a road junction.

Turn left here. Continue for 200 metres and then go right along a stony track just before a warning sign to traffic. Walk along the track and, just before the gates, turn left along a wide track. After 200 metres, the track twists left and right and finally turns left past an old stone house before reaching the road. The track is shown as two separate segments on the map but they link easily. The point of using this track is to avoid the main road for as long as possible. If, in the future, it is closed off, you will have to use the main road for your route – heeding the warning below. Also note that, whilst the map shows a track around Puig de Randa all the way to Randa, believe me that it is impossible!

Turn right at the road and walk towards Randa. **This is a busy road, so take great care**. Walk for 1km to a fork. Turn right here, passing point number 5 in the main directions and arrive in Randa.

Main route from Randa continues here

6. We now start the return section to Algaida. From the church in the centre of Randa, go downhill. Fork right just after the mill (Moli d'en Xim). Cross the main road to a quiet minor road then fork right (**2hrs 15mins**) and continue until you reach the road to Algaida (**2hrs 25mins**).

7. Walk along the road and, near to the 6km marker stone – and just past the entrance to "Puig de Son Redó" on your right – fork left (**2hrs 35mins**). Five minutes later, ignore a turn to the left and

continue on the main track. Finally join the road (**2hrs 55mins**) going all the way into Algaida (**3hrs 25mins**).

Other walks in the area

An information leaflet, available from the town hall in Algaida, provides brief details (in Spanish) of walks to Pina, Punxuat and Castellitx. It also includes considerable information about the history of Algaida.

Randa, at the mid-point of our walk, is most famous for the Sanctuary of Cura, associated with Ramon Llull, the Mallorcan mystic and philosopher – see Walk 1. Most modern-day pilgrims are making their way to the bar at the top of the hill or to a restaurant in the village, but you can walk up the minor road signposted to the sanctuary. After about 700 metres, the road bends sharp left and then back to the right; at this second sharp bend, a track shoots off to the left and leads up to the sanctuary.

Places of interest

Randa and **Castellitx** lie south-west of Algaida. **Llucmajor**, site of the defeat of Jaime III, is 10km south. Slightly further afield is the attractive town of **Montuiri** – about 8km from Algaida, towards Manacor. A helpful town hall has a leaflet in English, which tells you about Montuiri's 19 windmills, eight wells, its ancient crosses and the 16th-century church. Be sure to visit the excavated talayotic settlement at **Son Fornes**, 3.5km north-north-west of Montuiri. Son Fornes is most easily approached by heading north-west from Montuiri for 1km, turning right just after the 1km marker then, after 500metres, turn left. The site is on your right after 1.5km. It comprises the largest complete set of talayotic dwellings on the island, dating from 1000 BC. The most striking features are the two circular stone talayots with bases of 12-metre and 17-metre diameters. Visiting times are from Tuesday to Sunday from 10am to 2pm and 4pm to 8pm; admission (in 2008, including the museum) was 3.5 euros.

Further along the Manacor road, just after the km37 post on the way to Villafranca, you can visit **Els Calderes** – a 200-year-old farm with local products and a "living museum" of old Mallorca (see see www.elscalderers.com).

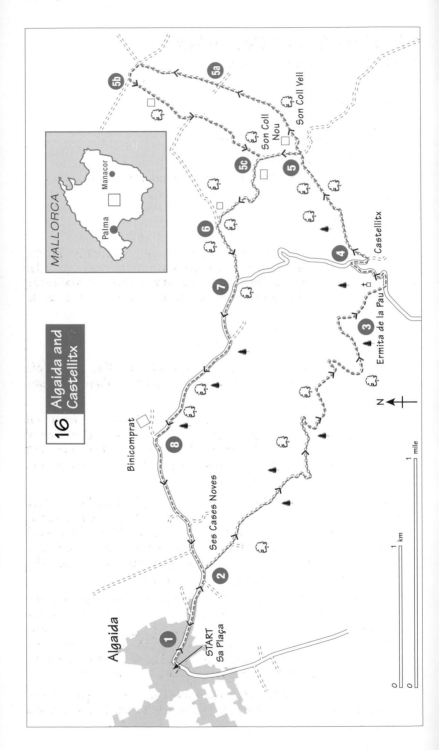

16. Algaida and Castellitx
A visit to a rural hermitage

Grade: easy
Distance: 10km or 12km
Time: 2½ to 3½ hours
Start & Finish: Algaida town centre
How to get there: see walk 15
Map: IGN 699/III (1:25,000 – see reference chart in introduction)
Checklist: walking boots; water; picnic; camera
Notes: see walk 15

This is the second of our walks from the charming old town of Algaida. It's a real eye-opener even to some who know the more popular walking routes: a mixture of woods, meadows and old Mallorcan hamlets – places where you're unlikely to meet another walker all day.

The Walk

Start in the main square of Algaida, perhaps with a coffee at the Café de's Poble – from where you can observe Mallorcan village life away from the tourist bustle.

1. At the bottom end of the square, diagonally across from our favoured café, walk along Carrer des Cavallers in the direction of the cemetery (*cementeri*) and the Guardia Civil. Turn right (**10 mins**) at the next "Cementeri" sign and pass the cemetery on your right. Soon, you enter beautiful woodland.

2. Fork right again (**15 mins**), then keep straight ahead on a track between stone walls. Continue along a track that winds gently uphill, taking a fork to the right soon after a track loops to the left (**20 mins**). From here, occasional red dots mark your route – just keep on the main forest track, ignoring all side turns. The track makes a wide loop to the right, then to the left.

3. Eventually (**50 mins**) descend to pass an old well on your right and cross a streambed lined with huge plane trees. Traverse a fertile cultivated area to a pair of green gates leading to a tarmac lane (**1hr**). Turn left and after just a few minutes you pass the hermitage of Ermita de la Pau (18th-century, but with parts dating from the 15th century) in the small hamlet of Castellitx.

4. After 50 metres a track makes a sharp hairpin to the right. Follow this and then, after another 20 metres, head north-east along a wide, stony track.

Ermita de la Pau, Castellitx

Can this really be Mallorca? It's like England with sunshine – or rural France (so I'm told).

Continue along this pleasant rural path until you come to a junction of paths and an abundance of "Coto Privado" (private hunting) signs.

5. You are now at San Coll Vell **(1hr 40mins)**. For the shorter walk, turn left through the gates and head north-west. If these gates are locked – or if you would like a slightly longer walk, here is an extra loop that adds half an hour or so to the main walk. The scenery is excellent and the additional effort is well rewarded.

Recommended Extension

Instead of turning left at the gates, walk ahead for a few metres and take a left fork. Pass an old farmhouse on the right, then turn left after passing a large threshing circle. Pass some ruins on your left and then go straight ahead where the track bends right.

The town way over to the right is Montuiri while in the distance, to the left, is the Tramuntana mountain range.

5a. After about 20 minutes from the farmhouse, go through some gates, past a couple of buildings and then a well.

5b. After a few more minutes, you come to a tarmac lane. Turn left here, then left again after 50 metres along a wide track running south-west, passing a large house on the right.

5c. At the next main junction, turn right and you are back on the main route.

Continuation of main (shorter) walk

Add 30 minutes to the following times if you have walked the longer route.

Our main route passes a stone building on the right and a track that leads to a building on the left. Keep going to a large wall and fence below houses **(1hr 55mins)**. Go left here, into the woods, on an uphill track.

6. At a T-junction **(2hrs 5mins)** turn left – there is a small building to your right.

   In the springtime there is an amazing variety of wildflowers in this area. You may also spot a tree with dark pink blossom: this is the Judas Tree, named from the legend that Judas Iscariot hanged himself from such a tree and, because of this, blushes with shame.

7 A few minutes later **(2hrs 15mins)** turn right towards the hamlet of Binicomprat and one of the many Mallorcan country estates called "possessions". This one, the Possessió Binicomprat, is now a beautifully situated Agroturismo that I am happy to recommend.

8 Keep left at Binicomprat and follow the lane back to Algaida – passing the pig farm along the way!

Other walks and places of interest

See walk 15.

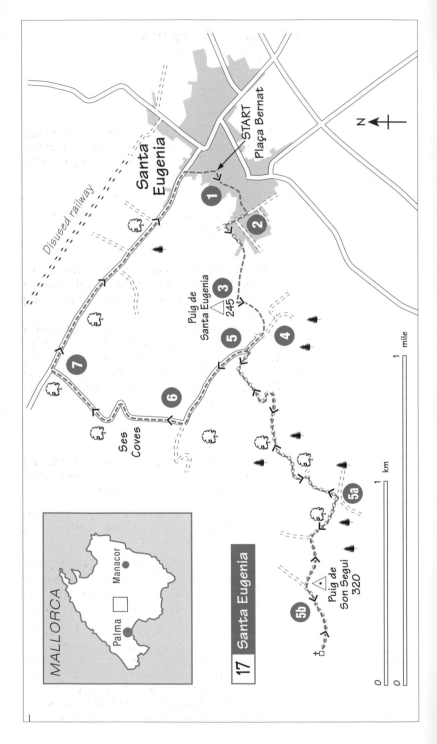

Santa Eugenia

START
Plaça Bernat

N

Disused railway

Puig de
Santa Eugenia
245

Ses
Coves

Puig de
Son Segui
320

MALLORCA

Manacor

Palma

17 Santa Eugenia

1 km

0

1 mile

0

17. Sant Eugènia
Three walks or one?

Grade: Moderate

Distance: 2.5km, 5km or 8.5km

Time: 1 to 3 hours

Start & Finish: Plaça Bernat de Santa Eugènia, in the centre of the village. No parking in the village centre but there is a car park in Carrer Josep Bulaguer, off Carrer des Sol, and on-street parking in general is not a problem.

How to get there: 10km along the Palma to Sineu road.

Map: IGN 699/I (1:25,000 – see reference chart in introduction)

Checklist: Walking boots; water; picnic; camera

So many choices: walk to the Puig de Santa Eugènia, enjoy the views, and return to the town, or continue for the whole circuit, with or without a visit to the old (ex-)hermitage on Puig d'en Marron (or Puig de Son Segui, as shown on maps).

Although there's a small town hall in Santa Eugènia, as yet there's no tourist office. The nearby parish church dates from the 16th century and marriages have taken place there since 1693. There are a number of prehistoric sites near Santa Eugènia and surrounding villages such as the hamlet of Ses Coves. For a brief history of Santa Eugénia, see www.a2zmallorca.com/detail/513.htm.

The Walk

Follow "Casa de l a Vila" signs to the main square – Plaça Bernat de Santa Eugènia – below the high tower of the parish church. There's the Bar C'an Prim, opposite the town hall, for refreshments.

1. Leave the square towards the Sa Nostra bank and turn left up Camí des Puig. Bear right at a "No through road" sign then climb steeply uphill and turn right on a wide, tarmac road.

2. At the end of the tarmac, turn sharp left to follow a path uphill, between two walls. Pass a red dot at the end of the wall on your right (do *not* turn here) then carry on uphill for another couple of minutes to a clear track on the right, again marked with a red dot.

   If you miss this turn you will get to the top of the hill and then need to retrace your steps. However, you may like to climb up anyway because, at the top there's a surprise: the remains of what looks like the front end of an aeroplane. How did it get there? Did it fall or was it placed? Thanks to Joe Miró Julia from the University in Mallorca, I have the answer: it's a submarine. Yes, really! It was built in about 1985 but it didn't work, so somebody decided to transport it, in sections, to the top of the mountain and convert it into a pub. That didn't work either, so there it – or what's left of it – remains. A few years ago it could be seen from far and wide but nowadays you have to walk there to see it.

Having turned right (at the red dot) off the main uphill track, follow a path to a gap in a wall **(20 mins)**. There are some stone steps on the left here, but you go straight ahead and up to the cross at the top of Puig de Santa Eugènia.

The submarine: original location

From here, there are excellent views of the village below and the mountains of the Tramuntana range to the north. If the weather is clear you should be able to spot Puig Mayor with its radar domes and, further left, the famed Alfàbia ridge with two sets of antennae stuck on the far left of the ridge.

3. Go back to the gap in the stone wall. **For the second half of the short walk**, go almost straight ahead and follow the red dots to retrace your steps back to Santa Eugénia. **For the longer versions** of the walk, go right after the gap and head down the stone steps.

    If you are continuing on one of the longer routes, and have turned right at the wall, as instructed, you should now pass through a prominent gap in the rocks. After this, turn right to follow the meandering path downhill and you soon come to a wire mesh fence.

    Follow the fence until it breaks away to the left. Continue ahead from here and head downhill. The path approaches a recently constructed house and turns left, then continues parallel to the drive with the fence on your immediate right. Where your path meets a wide stony track, turn right.

4. Continue along this wide track and join a slightly wider tarmac lane **(45 mins)**, where you turn right and pass the gates of Ca'n Elisita on your right.

5. After a further 150 metres you will see, on your left, a pair of iron gates – usually open, but in any case there's access to the left of them.

The hermitage diversion

This optional excursion takes about an hour.

Turn left at the iron gates, "Camino Particular" so far as vehicles are concerned. Walk up the winding tarmac track for 20 minutes until the track levels out, with a "Coto Privado de Caza" sign.

Along the way, pass an old well on your left and, a few minutes later, ornamental black swans on gateposts, which must surely be a first!

Turn right along a roughly stone-surfaced track on your right, the turn also being marked by a small cairn on the left. From here, continue on the obvious wide track. Do not turn left or right, however tempting the paths may seem – most lead to summer dwellings or farms.

After about five minutes, pass a castellated building surrounded by a wire fence – this is *not* the hermitage, so keep going!

Warning – the hermitage is not easy to find, so follow this next part carefully. Well-intended waymarks in the form of rough red outlines of a chapel are infrequent and only moderately accurate!

5a. A minute or so later, keep right at a large red arrow on a rock. Then keep uphill on the main track.

5b. This leads to a high wire fence, where you turn left, crossing a chain barrier and noting a small building on the left. Keep the fence on your right and pass a *huge* trig point marking the top of Puig d'en Marron/Son Segui (320m) and a still higher observation tower. Pass these on your left, then enter a wide clearing/picnic area at about the 30-minute mark.

Go to the far right-hand corner of the clearing and cross a gap in the wall. Just two minutes later, following a downhill path and keeping right at another clearing, you come to the entrance to the hermitage, with its well and three old wooden crosses.

Some restoration work has been done on this beautiful old building. It's a pity (though understandable) that the entrance is locked. However, walk over to the far side for a view of the grounds.

The Puig d'en Marron hermitage

Return from the hermitage by retracing your steps to the gap in the wall. Cross it and turn left to pass the trig point and observation tower on your right. Reach the wire fence and follow it round to the left, passing the small building and crossing the chain again. Ignore the track that you soon see on the left and, where you see the large red arrow, ignore the track on the right. Just follow the main track back to the tarmac, where you turn left and return downhill to the iron gates, where you turn left and pass Ca'n Vicens – it's tarmac all the way now.

Main route

Continue walking along the road. Add one hour to all the following times if you made the hermitage diversion.

6. At a junction (**55mins**), showing that you have walked along Comellà des Rafal, turn right to the hamlet of Ses Coves. Pass a well in the middle of the road and you will soon see, on your right, an iron gate (**1hr 10 mins**).

   The caves were used, so they say, to hide contraband. The gates tend to be locked nowadays.

   Go along the main village road. Ses Coves is a pleasant place with many well-restored buildings but there's not a lot to see – no church, not even a bar – so turn right and walk down to the main Ma-3040 road (**1hr 25mins**).

7. Unfortunately, there's no alternative but to turn right here and walk on the road for about 1km to Santa Eugènia.

   Along the road, pass "La Naranja Rosa", whose owner seems to enjoy painting his trees – well, he does have a lot of them!

   Take the first right turn into the village and return to the square by way of Carrer de Bisbe Sastre and Carrer Mayor.

Other Walks in the area

See Walks 15 and 16 for two walks from Algaida.

Places of interest

Sineu, 15km to the west, once had a royal palace, and still has many large and elegant old houses; on Wednesdays there is a large rural market. The railway station includes a contemporary art centre. **Binissalem's** many hectares of vines provide grapes for the some of the finest wines in Mallorca. Children will enjoy **Parc Natura** with its collection of animals, birds and plants. It lies about 1km south of Santa Eugènia on the Carretera de Sineu; tel 971 144078.

The view down Es Barranc towards Sóller (walks 27 and 28)

The North-West

18. Sóller town trail
Gateway to the mountains!

Grade: easy

Distance: 3km

Time: allow an entire morning or afternoon for this tour.

Start & Finish: Sóller's main square – Plaça de sa Constitució.

How to get there: the town is at the junction of the main roads from Palma, Pollença and Valldemossa. There are several car parks in Sóller. There's the famous train from Palma, the tram from Port de Sóller and buses from all directions.

Map: street maps and guides available from the tourist office (near the railway station) or local newsagents

Checklist: comfortable shoes; camera; money

Notes: most of the shops, many churches and the information office close in the afternoon. Also, the Botanical Garden is closed on Monday and on Sunday afternoons, while the Museum is closed on Sunday but open most of Monday!

As Sóller is the focal point for the walks in this section, a walk around the town seems appropriate. Although the main square is popular with tourists, the town itself is unspoilt – mainly because the streets are too narrow for buses. There is a great deal to see and many people will want to make several visits to this historic and charming town.

Sóller is a municipality comprising the town and its nearby port, together with a number of smaller villages such as Biniaraix. The name of the town is thought to be derived from the Arabic "sulliar", meaning "golden shell" – perhaps referring to its valley location. It certainly has a golden past, as it was at the heart of an exceptionally fertile and productive agricultural area.

The first steamship service between Mallorca and the mainland began in 1837, marking the beginning of a period of great prosperity for Sóller. During the second half of the 19th century oranges, almonds, olives, grapes and other crops were exported in huge amounts to the south of France. Many Mallorcan traders established successful distribution outlets in the south of France and became wealthy in the process - and some returned to build the impressive houses seen around the town. The historic trading ties with France also explain why French is still widely spoken around Sóller.

The period of prosperity ended with the loss of Spain's colonies, including Cuba, causing an abrupt decline in shipping and ship-building in the nearby port. To make things worse, the vines in the area were destroyed in 1890 by an attack of *Phylloxera*, but the resourceful people of Sóller began to grow different crops, tomatoes and oranges included, and latterly turned their attention to tourism – though not to any extent like the south of Mallorca.

Jaime I in the Plaça d'Espanya, Palma (Walk 1)

The Gran Hotel building, Palma (Walk 1)

The Es Foner statue, Palma (Walk 1)

Puig de Santa Eugenia (Walk 17)

The restored hermitage on Puig d'en Marron, near Santa Eugenia (Walk 17)

Torre d'Albarca – the 16th-century defensive tower on Cap Ferrutx (Walk 12)

Springtime near the monastery of Lluc (Walk 26)

The train at Sóller, about to leave for Palma (Walk 18)

Rural transport near Algaida (Walk 15)

One of Sóller's famous trams (Walk 18)

Olive groves and orange trees near Sa Figuera (Walk 19)

The Es Cornadors pass on the way to the Mirador de'n Quesada (Walk 29)

First sight of Sóller (Walk 18)

Street scene, Sóller (Walk 18)

The magnificent Banc de Sóller (Walk 18)

Olive trees and local resident above the bay of Port de Sóller (Walk 23)

The cloisters in the Convent des Sagrats Cors, Sóller (Walk 18)

Looking along the main street through Deià towards the parish church (Walks 22& 23)

Sa Foradada , ' the peninsula with a hole in it' – from the Archduke's bridleway (Walk 28)

Plaça de sa Constitució at the beginning of the 1900s: not a tourist in sight – but the very same water supply is still there. (Photograph: Foto Brasil)

The Walk

The Plaça de sa Constitució is the busy, colourful heart of Sóller. Soak up the atmosphere by having a drink at one of the bars.

The fountain in the centre of the square was commissioned in 1815 by Bishop Bernat Nadal, an important benefactor of the town.

1. First of all, walk to the huge parish church of St Bartholomew (Sant Bartomeu), which dominates the square.

   It was built in the late 17th and early 18th centuries on the site of a much smaller 14th-century church. The Art Nouveau façade was designed in 1904 by Joan Rubió i Bellver, a follower of Gaudí. Inside, there is an impressive high altar and a beautiful stained-glass rose window. The side chapels have numerous Gothic and Baroque altars and other features. Festival week, to commemorate St Bartholomew, is at the end of August.

   To the left of the church is the impressive Bank of Sóller building, now a branch of Banco Santander. The bank was established in 1889, thanks to fortunes made overseas by returning emigrants. The building was designed in the Modernist style by Rubió in 1909 and construction started in 1912.

   The town hall, with its wide sweep of stone steps, is to the right of the church. Follow the tram track, to the right of the town hall, up Carrer des Born and through the Plaça de España.

   The tram service (Tranvia de Sóller) has been operating between Sóller and the port, some 5km away, since October 1913. The first three trams were constructed on the Spanish mainland and, many

The train from Palma arriving at Sóller soon after inauguration of the service in 1912 (photograph: Foto Brasil)

years later, five more were purchased from Lisbon. It was the first – and remains the only – tram service on Mallorca. Don't believe anybody who tells you that the trams came from San Francisco. Visit http://www.simplonpc.co.uk/T_Majorca-2.html to read its history and to see an excellent collection of photographs.

As you walk up here, you pass Soller's tourist information centre, suitably located in a restored mail wagon from the town's railway company, established in 1912 by Jeroni Estades.

2. At the top of this street, just past the Bar el Tren, is Sóller's train station, complete with a plaque in honour of its founder.

The building is based on the 17th-century property of Ca'n Mayol. In the station buildings there are permanent exhibitions of ceramics by Picasso and paintings by Miró. Captions are terse and there are no descriptions of the exhibits, but you can't complain as there is no admission charge.

Go up the steps to the platform and a train may be in the station for you to inspect at close quarters. The carriages are much the same as when the railway opened on 16th April 1912. It connects Sóller with Palma, just 27km away (http://www.simplonpc.co.uk/ T_Majorca-1.html).

Come back out of the station and, heading downhill, go to the left side of Plaça de España and turn left along Carrer d'Isabel II.

3. Continue along this road.

On the left you pass the hotel Ca'n Isabel, soon followed by the birthplace (note the plaque) of Guillem Colom i Casasnovas, a

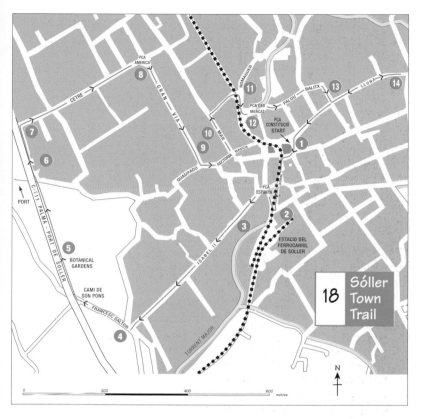

18 Sóller Town Trail

Mallorcan naturalist, and a succession of posadas (mini-palaces), including the balconied Posada de Montnàber (house number 37) with its prominent plaque to the poet Guillem Colom i Ferrà.

Continue walking along the street until you reach a junction and a pedestrian crossing.

4. Here, turn right up some steps into Placeta de Francesc Saltor to the Convent des Sagrats Cors (18th century), which is usually open – a peaceful place after the bustle of Sóller's busy centre. Come out of the church and look back to see the large plaque relating to Saint Junipero Serra, born in Petra, Mallorca, in 1713. See Walk 10 for more details of this energetic evangelist.

    Continue down the steps and turn left down Camí de Son Pons. This leads to the main Sóller-Palma road. Turn right here.

5. You soon come to the Botanical Garden and the Museum of Natural Sciences. Open Tue – Sat, 10:00 – 18:00; Sundays/Public Holidays 10:00 – 14:00; Closed Monday; Entrance fee (2008) €5.

    I have met very few people who have visited the gardens – those who don't are missing a treat! If you can't read Spanish, ask for a leaflet in English. The museum is located in buildings that were part of the Ca'n Prohom estate. Upstairs, there is a permanent exhibition depicting the natural history of the Balearic Islands, from their formation some 150 million years ago. Outside, you can stroll around the gardens for an hour or more. In addition to the huge range of flowers, shrubs and trees (about 500 species) there is an area devoted to the traditional fruits of Mallorca.

6. After your visit, continue down the main road, pass the petrol station on the right and then the Ca'n Lluis bar – this could be a good time for a break.

7. Continue the tour by walking along the main road for a further 50 metres and then turn right along Carrer de Cetre. This takes you past the bus terminus (for Palma and Port de Sóller) and into the Plaça de America.

   There's a pleasant bar, an old monument, some benches in the centre and Ca'n Cetre, a balconied old building of faded elegance across one corner of the square.

8. Turn right to walk up Gran Via. Along this street, there are many impressive buildings showing baroque and Art Nouveau influences. On the right, behind wrought iron gates, number 27 is unusual as it is built partly of red brick. Shortly after, on the left, is Ca'n Cremat, built in 1920 in neo-Classical style complete with pillars.

   On the right is Ca'n Dulce – the Sóller cultural centre where many evening classes and small exhibitions are held. With luck, the doors will be open, so go in and admire the interior.

   Further up and on the left is Ca'n Canals – not open to the public. On the right is the up-market L'Avenida Hotel, serving a 'poolside lunch'.

9. Near the top of the street (just after the car park on the left) look through a grille to a patio decorated with the work of local modern artisans. You can also visit the shop.

   The last house of note in Gran Via, at the top of the street and on the right, is the old rectory. There are now two options:

10a **Shorter but busier:** Turn left at the top of Gran Via, along Carrer de la Rectoria, and pass, on your right, Casa de los Hermanos de la Caridad (House of the Brothers of Charity) with its stone archway and nearby plaque. Continue a short distance along Carrer de Bauca, past the post office, and turn left at the "Museu" sign down Carrer de Mar.

10b **Longer but more interesting:** This takes you through a maze of medieval streets. Having passed the old rectory at the top of Gran

Via, turn right up Carrer Josep M Quadrada. After about 50m, on the right is an entrance to "Garage Ca'n Pelut". Peep down here, noting the stone passageway and arches. Continue uphill along Carrer de Tamany, Calle de Jesus, and Carrer de Volta Piquera, eventually passing Hotel Ca'l Bisbe – part of which was Bishop Nadal's residence. Turn left at the road, Carrer Isabella II (which we've walked along before). After 100m, go left down Carrer de Sant Antoni, right along Crostóbal Pizá, then first left down Carrer de la Murta and left again at Carrer del Vicari Pastor. You cross the busy shopping street of Carrer de Bauca into Carrer de Mar.

Whichever way you took, this road leads to the town's museum – an essential visit, but note the advertised opening times: Mon – Fri, 11:00 – 16:00, Saturday 11:00 – 13:00; Closed on Sunday – and whenever they feel like it, or so it seems. However, you should avoid both Sunday and Monday to get the best out of this tour – because the botanical gardens are closed on Monday, not Sunday! Admission in 2008 was €2. A printed guide can be borrowed, but only in Spanish or German, and in any case it was badly out of date in 2008, so here are some of the highlights:

The Sóller Museum – a brief guide for visitors

The building is based on a 1740 house and garden which, in 1958, were restored and adapted for use as a museum. In August 2000, a grant of approximately 5000 euros was used to restore the roof and, by 2008, there had been considerable enhancements and enlargements, including rooms for exhibitions and events.

On the left, past the pay desk, there is a modern function room with several interesting old photographs. Back in the entrance hall there are various religious items – including altar panels and sculptures from a Franciscan Convent that was demolished in 1945. On the wall on the right, as you enter the entrance hall, you will see the oldest-known town plan of Sóller, dated 1858. Also on the right, there is a restored old **kitchen** with household furniture and cooking utensils typical of the area. Towards the back of the museum there is a display of rural items including carriage lanterns, woodworking tools, and a 16th-century workbench. The attractive **courtyard** has a well, a collection of stonework, old street signs from the town, a huge anchor and architectural remains.

On the mezzanine floor, a **dining room** is furnished with a mulberry table and 19th-century chairs. There is a collection of 19th-century Catalan crystal in the sideboard at the back of the room.

Continue upstairs to the first floor. At the top of the stairs, there are examples of pottery from the "La Roquetra" factory of Palma (1897-1918). Go up a few steps and turn right into what was once a bedroom, now housing a small **archaeological exhibition** donated by Guillem Bernat Crespi and AntoniEstades. The connecting room (Sala Paul Haefliger) has a collection of **ritual masks** from Papua New Guinea. Further on is another function room.

Disused textile mill by the river just below the Plaça dels Teixidors car park (photo: Iain Williamson)

Go back through the archaeological collection to a **natural history** room with paintings of flowers and dried or pressed flowers, the work of Colette Martin and botanist Jeroni Orell; the next, central room contains paintings by Mallorcan artists and furniture including chairs upholstered with bulrushes in the Catalan tradition and a splendid large chair constructed for the arrival in Sóller of King Alfonso XII. At the time of writing (October 2008), in the centre of this room – heaven knows why – there was an antique yarn strength tester, made by John Nesbitt of Market Street, Manchester. As I live just a few miles from Manchester, this was interesting – though it ought to be on the top floor with other items of the cotton trade. Sóller, together with a few other towns in Mallorca, once had a flourishing textile trade and woven products were an important part of the island's economy.

Pass from here to the **bedroom,** on the right-hand side, there is a cherrywood chest of drawers, a jewellery box, and a display case decorated with religious symbols, all from the 19th century. The wide, wooden item with a central metal bowl is a *brasero* – glowing embers were placed in it so that you could warm your feet on a wintry night.

There is a small **chapel**, which includes a statuette of the Virgin of the Sorrows, venerated in a procession on Easter Sunday morning.

On the top floor there is an **exhibition hall** with collections of musical instruments, clothing, photography and pottery. There are various documents relating to trade with, and migration to, Puerto Rico. A balcony is accessible from the main room, leading also to a separate room with an old printing press and a plate camera that might have been used in the printing industry. A collection of paintings dated 1880 show how small Sóller was at that time.

Before the recent development of the museum there used to be a 100-peseta note on display; it was issued by the Bank of Sóller and measured 12 inches by 9 inches. Ask the museum staff where it is!

Town Trail, continued

Come out of the museum, turn left and continue down the street; then turn right into the attractive narrow paved street of Carrer de la Romaguera.

11. This leads you to the public market – worth browsing to see (and buy!) the local produce. The market is open Monday to Saturday, 9am to 1pm and there is also a travelling market, with stalls between here and the main square, every Saturday from 8am to 1pm.

To the left of the market is the Gran Hotel Sóller. The original building dates to 1880, and was the home of the local Casasnovas family. In the 1960s, it was converted into a hotel but, though initially successful, was unable to compete with the big hotel chains during 1970s mass tourism. It remained closed for many years but was rescued, thanks to the vision of Andres Galabert, an American citizen who was born in Sóller. It reopened in 2004 as a 5-star hotel, having retained much of the original architecture and is a great credit to its developers. At the very least, do call in for morning coffee or afternoon tea.

Almost opposite the market you will see the Sóller Ice Cream shop and open-air café, and the 'Fet a Sóller' shop selling other local products.

12. Continue the walk by taking the street (Carrer de Palou) on the right of the market, with the river below and to the left. Ignore the right turn to Carrer de Serra, but cross Carrer de la Victoria 11 Maig and continue to the end of Carrer Bailitx, passing the 18th-century Posada de Bailitx (number 7) on your left. (Bailitx is a small village outside Sóller.)

You will come across many references to the 11th May (Maig) in Sóller. This relates to the successful resistance by the people of the town to an attempted invasion in 1561 by the Turkish pirate Otxali and a force of 1,700 men. The event is marked by the Monument to the May Martyrs (at the junction of the road from the port and the Ma-10) and with an absolutely amazing and very noisy annual festival, during which the invasion is re-enacted at the port and with mock battles between the Christians and Moors until the crescendo in the Plaça de sa Constitució. This is not for those of a nervous disposition: thousands of rounds of blank ammunition and hundreds of noisy fireworks explode. The Moors lose every time, of course.

13. As the narrow road turns to the right, you pass the late 18th-century Iglesia de la Sangre, or Church of the Sacred Heart.

The alleyway leads you to Carrer de la Lluna – "Moon Street". As you join this famous street with its mixture of modern and traditional shops, immediately opposite is the medieval Casa de la Lluna; look up and you'll see a relief of the moon on the wall.

Turn left for a short walk down the street. Pass, on your right, the small side street of Carrer de Pons and you soon come to one of Sóller's most famous buildings – the lavishly Art Nouveau Ca'n Prunera, built in 1911 with contrasting stonework and wrought iron (being renovated in 2008).

From here, turn back and continue along Carrer de la Lluna until you are back in the Plaça de sa Constitució.

For years, the only problem with Carrer de la Lluna has been the traffic, but funding is now in place for pedestrianisation – scheduled for 2009.

Looking from Carrer de la Lluna to Sóller's main

Other walks in the area

There are so many! Possibilities include: Deià by the Camino de Castelló (reverse of Walk 20): Biniaraix to Es Cornadors (see Walk 27); Sa Figuera to the port (see Walk 19). A book of local walks is available from the tourist information office near the railway station.

Places of interest

Port de Sóller: go there by tram – one of the best parts of the journey is just a few minutes down the track as you pass the back gardens of Sóller, full of orange and lemon trees. **Ses Tres Creus** (the three crosses) is a monument that commemorates the time when church relics were stored in a nearby small cave during the Moorish occupation; it's in the hillside above the town cemetery, the latter being justifiably famous for its ornately decorated tombs, headstones and marble angels. **Biniaraix** is a small, quaint village with stepped streets while **Fornalutx** is another "old Mallorca" village, though one that gets busier every year, just a short drive by car or local bus, or a very pleasant walk via Biniaraix of about an hour."

19. Port de Sóller to Sa Figuera
Heroes and Oranges

Grade: easy/moderate

Distance: 7km

Time: 2½ hours

Start & Finish: Port de Sóller

How to get there: catch a tram at any of the stops in Port de Sóller.

Map: IGN 670/II (1:25,000 – see reference chart in introduction)

Checklist: walking boots; water; picnic; camera; money

This is another excuse for a tram ride, with wonderful views and the bonus of fresh orange juice in the garden of a splendid old Mallorcan farmhouse.

Note: if you prefer not to use the tram, there is a very pleasant path from the Repic beach in the port. It goes past the old Rocamar hotel and towards Sóller, parallel to the road and on the seaward side of the river – the tram running between the two. Do *not* follow the GR221 sign as this does *not* take you on our intended route. The path that you should follow eventually crosses the river, then continues for a short distance towards Sóller to a pedestrian crossing over the main road. Cross over here and continue a bit further to a waymarked tarmac lane on the left, which takes you directly to the Lluc side of the roundabout – at the end of point 1 in the following direction.

The Walk

1. If using the tram, get off at the roundabout connecting the Ma-11 road from the port with the Ma-10 to Lluc and Pollença and cross the road to the huge pottery shop.

    Ask the conductor to stop at "El Monumento" – or pull the cord when you're approaching the roundabout. The "Monument to the May Heroes" was erected in 1971 to commemorate the resistance of Sóller to an attempted invasion of Berber (Turkish) pirates on 11th May 1561.

    Those who walk from the port also arrive at the pottery shop. Whichever way you got here, start walking below the Ma-10 in the direction of Lluc and Pollença. There's a classic view of Sóller to your right – the first of many photo-opportunities.

2. Follow the waymarks and after just 300 metres (**7 mins**), you'll see a sign pointing left to "Finca Ca'n Penya" at the start of a minor road called Camí de Ca'n Tamany. Turn left and walk along this tarmac lane, with well-kept gardens to either side.

After 200 metres, turn left at a Ca'n Penya sign (and Port de Sóller signpost) and pass the small house called Ca'n Tamany.

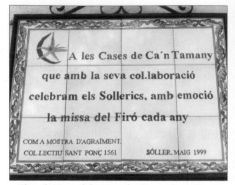

The plaque celebrating the Casasnovas sisters

This was the home of two Mallorcan sisters, Francisca and Catalina Casasnovas. In 1561, an opportunistic Moslem force of 1,700 men under the command of a Turk called Otxali landed in the port and made their way inland. Their progress was fiercely resisted by the people of Sóller, and particularly by the two sisters who not only protected their own honour and dignity, but also managed to kill several of the invaders. A plaque on the wall of the house tells us that the people of Sóller "commemorate the bravery of the houses of Ca'n Tamany every year at the Firò mass".

Continue walking along the track and then **(20mins)** fork left on a narrower path, as indicated by a waymark. This, referred to as the 'Antic camí de Sa Figuera', would have been the original path over the Coll d'en Borrassà pass to the port.

3. The footpath winds uphill and crosses the vehicle track **(25mins)** with another sign to Port de Sóller. Follow the cobbled path and you soon rejoin the main track, still heading uphill.

At a three-way sign **(30mins)** indicating 30 minutes back to Sóller (optimistic if they mean the town centre), 30 minutes to Port de Sóller by forking left (about right) and 50 minutes also to the port by going straight ahead – this last one is the way we are going today.

If you're weary, and prepared to forsake fresh orange juice in the garden of Ca'n Bardi, try the left fork. We walked it for the first time in 2008 and it's a very pleasant alternative. Waymarking is good and there are some interesting sights along the way, including an ancient (Moorish?) irrigation channel and, at the bottom end where the path emerges near to a portal of the new tunnel, a reconstructed lime kiln and a rather odd stone tunnel-like construction – no description yet available.

For the full walk, continue uphill, ignoring turns to left and right, and pass through a gateway with (in 2008) a 'Privado' sign attached to the wide steel gate. This only applies to vehicles; as confirmation, just a few metres further on there's a sign offering fresh orange juice to walkers!

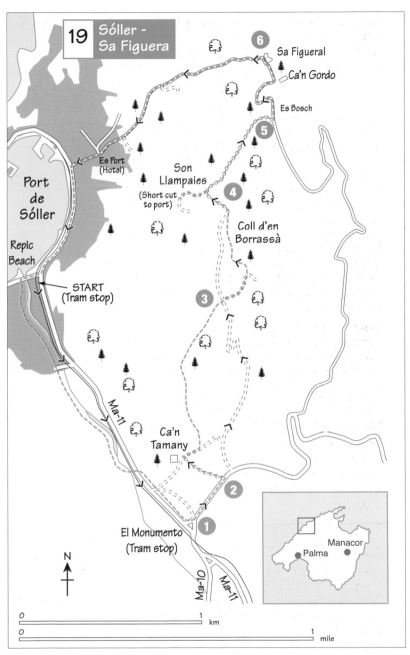

19 Sóller - Sa Figuera

Sa Figueral

Ca'n Gordo

Es Bosch

6

5

Port de Sóller

Es Port (Hotel)

Son Llampaies

(Short cut to port)

4

Coll d'en Borrassà

Replc Beach

3

START (Tram stop)

Ma-11

Ca'n Tamany

2

1

El Monumento (Tram stop)

Ma-10 Ma-11

N

Manacor

Palma

0   1
                     km

0   1
                     mile

4. Close the gate behind you, as requested, walk past the houses (**45 mins**) of Son Llampalles and soon you see some interesting remains of what looks like a double side-by-side lime kiln, though not of the usual Mallorcan design.

Continue along the main route, ignoring any turns to the right. Go through a second gate and walk amongst attractive olive groves with photogenic views of the Port of Sóller.

5. At a T-junction (**1hr**) turn left onto a tarmac road and pause to admire the splendid estate of Es Bosch across the valley.

What a beautiful, fertile area this is and what wealth it created for its owners – olives, almonds and oranges all still grow here in abundance. One of the main markets used to be southern France – photographs taken in France in the early part of the 20th century show shopkeepers proudly displaying their Mallorcan produce.

Continue downhill, with the estates of Ca'n Gordo and Ca S'Heret coming into view. At **1hr 15min** and after a total distance of 500 metres from the T-junction mentioned at the start of direction (5) above, you come to a large house called "Ca'n Bardi" surrounded by the orange groves of Sa Figuera. Walking in this direction, it is easy to miss the sign for oranges ('naranjas') and, even if you do spot the sign, it doesn't *actually* say that there's orange *juice* for sale – but there is (along with other irresistible local products).

There's a huge sundial on the outside wall and tables and chairs dotted about in the garden: a beautiful place to relax for a while. And here's a tip: be sure to go inside the entrance hall of this fabulous old house where there's a tempting display of goodies on sale. While you are there, ask if you can see the small but beautiful private chapel and perhaps the collection of old agricultural equipment, including an olive press that is still in use. The history of the building stretches back over 500 years – long before the historic stand of the spirited Casasnovas sisters!

6. From here, it's a 2km downhill stroll and then a walk on the level back to Port de Sóller, laden with almonds, olives and marmalade from Sa Figuera! The finish time depends on how long you stayed at Ca'n Bardi.

Other walks in the area

In addition to the walks in this book, the walk from the port to the Torre Picada watchtower is a pleasant hour-long circular. From the Generoso Hotel in Port de Sóller, walk along Almirante Abarzusa street and then uphill to the headland, noting progress on the Sa Talaia hotel: building started in 1996, was stalled, but completion to super-luxury status is said to be scheduled for 2010.

Places of interest

There is a pleasant beach at the port, and a marina with a wide range of boats. Trips can be booked from here to many destinations, including Cala Deià and Sa Calobra.

20. Sóller, the port and the GR221

Grade: easy
Distance: 8km
Time: 2½ hours
Start and finish: Sóller's main square – Plaça de sa Constitució
How to get there: See Walk 18
Map: IGN 670/II (1:25,000 – see reference chart in introduction)
Checklist: walking boots; money for refreshments; water; picnic; camera
Note: for sketch map, see Walk 19

No trams this time, just a short and easy 'taster' of the GR221 – Mallorca's premier walking route. It takes only a couple of hours or so if you don't stop along the way, but there's plenty to see – and the bars and cafés in the town and port are bound to prove just too tempting!

The Walk

Leave the square along Carrer de sa Lluna and take the second left down Carrer de La Victoria "11 Maig", marked with the first of many GR221 signs. Follow this road which eventually becomes Avinguda d'Asturies.

1. Pass the football stadium (do not continue right at the GR221 sign) and continue along Camí de ses Argiles to a right fork (**15 mins**), signed to Port Sóller and Poliesportiu. Fork right again, now on a two-way street and continue to a T-junction with the main Ma-10 road, which you cross.

2. Pass a signpost to the port and continue on the Camí de ses Alzines, following the waymark posts. At a tarmac lane, turn right to follow the sign to the port and continue uphill to a waymark by a telegraph pole. This leads to the old route to the port used in the walk 19, so follow the cobbled path uphill and you soon rejoin the main track, still heading uphill.

3. At the three-way sign (**40mins**), turn left to Port de Sóller. The route from here is well waymarked and there are some interesting sights along the way, including ancient (Moorish?) irrigation channels

4. The path emerges near to a portal of the new tunnel. Pass a reconstructed lime kiln and a rather odd stone tunnel-like construction – no description yet available. Continue from here to the port (**1hr 10mins**). After a mooch around, follow the pedestrianised section of the Ma-11 towards Sóller.

5. At the end of the bay, turn right with the Repic beach on your right

Promenade alongside Repic beach, Port de Sóller

and cross a bridge over the *torrent*. Walk past the shops and bars to a telephone box and the Los Geranios hotel. Turn left here and keep walking along the road, passing the Campo-Sol restaurant.

You soon approach the driveway to the old Rocamar hotel (as mentioned elsewhere, this has been semi-derelict for years but was still standing in 2008).

6. Walk about 100m past the hotel building **(1hr 25 mins)** to an information board showing the GR221 going uphill and to the right for the Refugi de Muleta or straight ahead to Sóller. This time, be sure to go straight ahead.

   From here, the GR221 to Sóller is well-waymarked and needs scarcely any further description. After climbing around a deep ravine, there are some excellent views towards Sóller and its encircling mountains.

7. The route eventually crosses the Ma-10 from Deia, then the Ma-11 (Palma via tunnel road) and takes you all the way to Plaça de sa Constitució in the centre of Sóller.

Other walks in the area

See Walks 18 and 19.

Places of Interest

Thanks to the new tunnel around the port area, there has been rapid development in the past few years. The sea-front is mainly

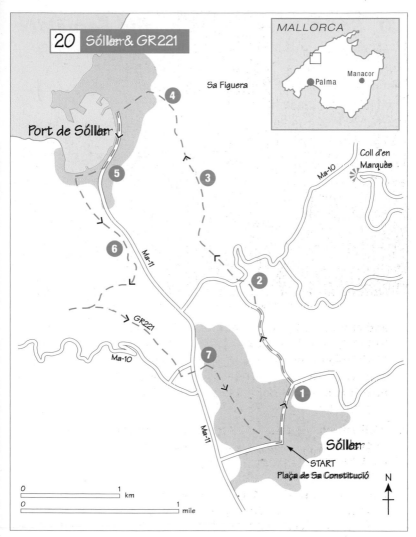

20 Sóller & GR221

MALLORCA

Palma · Manacor

Sa Figuera

Port de Sóller

Coll d'en Marques

Ma-10

Ma-11

GR221

Ma-10

Ma-11

Ma-11

START
Plaça de Sa Constitució

Sóller

0   1
km

0   1
mile

N

pedestrianised, except for trams and vehicles using the hotels – so don't assume that there's no traffic. There is a smart new marina, which may soon compete with Andratx and, eventually, even with Palma. At the northern end of the bay, a visit to the Museum of The Sea is worthwhile. Open Tuesday to Saturday, entrance €3 in 2008.

21. Sóller to the Mirador and Fornalutx
A chapel, a bar and a popular mountain village

Grade: moderate

Distance: 10km

Time: just over 3 hours, including stops

Start and finish: Sóller's main square – Plaça de sa Constitució

How to get there: See Walk 18.

Map: IGN 670/II (1:25,000 – see reference chart in introduction)

Checklist: walking boots; money for refreshments; water; picnic; camera

Notes: The outward route is on the strenuous side of moderate, as it climbs all the way to the Mirador. If it all becomes a bit too much you can cut it short by, for example, heading for Port de Sóller (signed) less than half-way round or catching a bus back from Fornalutx, though it's all downhill from there!

This splendid walk has many attractions: a tiny chapel that would be more at home in Barcelona; a famous 'mirador; a visit to a popular mountain village and glimpses of Mallorca's Moorish past.

A 'mirador' is a 'viewpoint' and one of the best on the whole island is the Mirador de Ses Barques, visited on this walk. When we were here in 2008, we met a charming couple from Cologne. The husband told us how he loved the view – and we learned that he had more reason than most to enthuse about it as he had just spent six days in Palma hospital, being treated for a heart condition. According to his wife, this was to be the last time he would see this splendid view, giving us all the more reason to enjoy every minute of our walk.

The Walk

Leave the square along Carrer de sa Lluna and take the second left down Carrer de La Victoria "11 Maig", marked with a GR221 sign. Follow this road which eventually becomes Avinguda d'Asturies.

1. Turn right at the football stadium. Go up Camí des Murterar, over the Pont de Ca'n Rave and left at the information board – still following GR221 signs – and, then right up an unnamed road (**10mins**).

2. Just 70 paces up this road, opposite to a house called "Villa Ideal", turn left up a track signposted to "Tuent, Sa Colabra and Cami de Capelleta" – make sure that you do use this track.

   Turn left at a wider vehicular track (**15mins**) and almost immediately right at a gap in the wall, to begin a steady climb on a narrower, stony track with occasional waymarks. This crosses the

The Capelleta

vehicle track at several places, effectively cutting out the loops, passing several properties including Ca'n Perus and Ca'n Eugenio.

3. Eventually, reach a track and gateway on the right to a religious centre **(40 mins)**. For a more interesting – and stranger – building, go left past a large wooden cross and through a gate to the Capelleta de Sant Maria.

   Said to be in Modernist style, the surrounding walls are decorated with higgledy-piggledy piles of stones, while the chapel itself resembles a scene from a Grimm's fairy tale or a Tolkien fantasy.

   Leave the *capelleta* and go up a path from the gateway to the main road (Ma-10 to Lluc). Cross straight over here and continue up the stepped track. The route continues uphill with waymarks and occasional signs still pointing to Tuent.

4. At about **1hr 5mins**, reach a waymark pointing left to Port de Sóller; this is worth remembering if you need to cut the walk short and there is also a sign on your right to Fornalutx. Our way is straight ahead (signed to Tuent and Sa Costera) – a ladder stile can be seen opposite, but avoid wall damage by going right for a few metres then left to the stile and gate – again signed to Tuent and Sa Costera.

   Follow waymarks up and through the terraces, then pass through another gate and further uphill to a waymark opposite stone steps **(1hr 15mins)**.

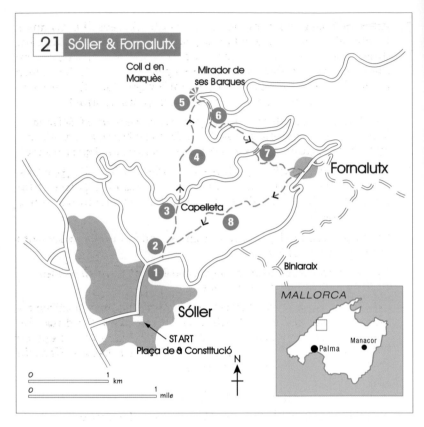

21 Sóller & Fornalutx

Coll d en
Marquès

Mirador de
ses Barques

5

6

4

7

Fornalutx

3 Capelleta

8

2

1

Biniaraix

MALLORCA

Sóller

START
Plaça de a Constitució

Manacor

Palma

N

0   1
        km
0   1
            mile

5. A final climb alongside a steel protective cable takes you to the
    Mirador de Ses Barques **(1hr 30mins)**.

    There's a lookout point from where you can admire the view over Port
    de Soller, and the view is just about as good from the open-air
    terrace restaurant below.

    After a 15-minute break, leave the Mirador and retrace your steps
    alongside the steel cable for a few minutes to a three-way sign and
    turn left, signed as 55 minutes to Fornalutx. This is the start of a
    downhill stony track, stepped in parts, that crosses the Ma-10
    main road from Sóller at several places – it clearly existed long
    before the Ma-10.

6. The first crossing is signed to "Costa den Nicó and Fornalutx" and,
    100m down the Ma-10 fork left (same destinations) and then fork
    right, downhill at "Fornalutx a Peu" **(1hr 55mins)**. There are more
    crossings of the Ma-10 and, each time you re-join the track be
    sure to follow the occasional waymarks and cairns, often cutting
    loops off wider tracks that, while also leading in the right general
    downhill direction, will take longer.

7. After the final crossing of the main road, track leads directly down to Fornalutx, passing a retaining wall on the left and dropping down to a T-junction with Carrer de La Pau. At this junction, note the house name behind you: "Can Puig de Ros, No 6". You return to this later but for now, turn left, then right along Carrer de sa Plaça, into the main square of Fornalutx (**2hrs 35mins**).

The village, of Moorish origins, only became independent of Sóller in 1837. It is now a popular day-visit and firmly on the tourist trail. For historic background, see www.mallorcaweb.com/reports/villages/fornalutx/

After a 15-minute break, retrace your steps to "Can Puig de Ros, No 6" and – this time – go straight on, passing a footpath sign for Sóller and Binibassí. Pass the cemetery and continue on a concrete path.

8. Keep right at a steel gate (**2hrs 50mins**) and follow waymarks into the tiny hamlet of Binibassí.

Again of Moorish origins, the village consists of just a few houses and has ancient irrigation channels.

Continue downhill to a tarmac lane where you must turn right – the tempting path ahead leads only to properties. Go down the lane, passing Villa Ideal again (**3hrs**) and retrace your steps by following the GR221 signs in reverse, all the way back to Plaça de sa Constitució in the centre of Sóller.

Other walks in the area

See notes at end of Walk 18 and other walks in this section.

Places of Interest

Fornalutx was, not so long ago, a sleepy mountain village. Nowadays, it is becoming a popular destination for coach parties, but there are still some quiet corners to explore. The town hall has a 17th-century defensive tower, while the parish church is originally 13th century, though with many renovations. There is a tradition of painted rooftiles in the village – see www.firstmallorca.com/ru/fornalutx.

22. Deià to Sóller
The Postman's Path

Grade: easy

Distance: 12km

Time:3 hours

Start: on the Ma-10, 2km from Deià in the direction of Sóller, opposite the entrance to the property called Finca Ca'n Puig Server.

How to get there: there is only a very small amount of roadside parking (room for only one car) near to the start point, so my suggestion is to get a taxi from Sóller or Deià to the entrance to Ca'n Puig Server – this avoids a hazardous walk along the Ma-10.

Second best is to catch a bus to Deià: there's one from Sóller at about 09:25 but it's often packed with walking groups from Port de Sóller and you may have to catch a later one. From Palma, there is a bus at 10:00 (summer and winter), arriving in Deià at 10:45. From the bus stop, the safest option is to walk along the Ma-10 in the Sóller direction to the outskirts of the village and turn left at the GR221 sign. This takes you down a well-waymarked route through olive groves, along a tarmac lane (access to Cala Deià) and up a final rough track to the Ma-10. From here continue **with great care** for 500m to the next "GR" sign on the right, and cross the road to a stepped path, about 50m or so before Ca'n Puig Server.

How to get back: buses leave Port de Sóller for Deià at 15:30 and 17:30 (Mon-Sat) and at 14:30 and 18:30 (Sun) from Carrer de L'Esglesia (or, a minute or so later, from the Sa Torre bus stop at the car park near Platja d'en Repic) and ten minutes later from the Sóller bus terminus in Carrer de Cetre, near to Plaça de America. Check the current timetable and be sure to catch the L210, not the L200 'Tunel' service.

Map: IGN 670/II (1:25,000 – see reference chart in introduction)

Checklist: walking boots or trainers; money for bus fares and refreshments; water; picnic; camera; bus timetable.

Notes: this is one of the very few linear routes in this book; the bus services are reliable but infrequent, so be sure to check the timetable before you set off. If you're using a car, aim to start the walk at about 10am, then you'll be able to enjoy a drink or lunch in Sóller and catch an early afternoon Port de Sóller/Sóller to Deià service – so long as you keep to the schedule described. If you arrive by bus from the Palma direction, you'll be under a little more pressure, but relax – there's plenty to occupy you in Sóller if you have to return on a later bus.

Much of this walk follows the old mule route all the way from Deià to Sóller. This was the main track for traders and travellers before the

Ma-10 was built, so locals still refer to it as the Postman's Path. The track used to start from the centre of Deià, but the first 2km have been lost due to residential development. Along the way, there are shady paths, panoramic views and even some culture to soak up.

Going in this direction is preferable to the reverse – you'll be walking downhill most of the time and can have a chuckle to yourself as you spot the nationalities of the perspiring walkers on their way up from Sóller – 'Guten Tag', 'Buenos Dias', 'Bonjour' . . .

The Walk

The entire route is now well-waymarked with rustic fingerposts. This is excellent news, even if some of the detailed directions are not so necessary. Note that timings are from the entrance to Ca'n Puig Server, not from Deià.

1. From Ca'n Puig Server, walk up the wide metalled track opposite to the entrance until you reach a "Sóller-Deià" sign on the wall and a small cairn to mark the start. Alternatively, walk from Ca'n Puig Server towards Deià for about 50 metres to a stepped track that will be used by those who have walked the GR221 route from Deià.

    In either case, climb the rocky path until it levels out **(15 mins)** with the first of several views of the hamlet of Lluc Alcari nestling in the woods below, and the sparkling blue sea beyond.

2. Follow the gently rising slope which takes you past a small house on the left.

    About here, on the right, there used to be an unusual collection of wind-animated and other sculptures – there were no explanations, it just seemed to be somebody's hobby!

    The scenery becomes more open, with olive terraces and the sounds of grazing sheep and goats – their bells as much in evidence as their bleating.

3. Descend some steps **(30 mins)** to a junction of paths where there are iron gates to the left. Be sure to keep to the right. About a minute later you come to another junction which you cross over and continue up rocky steps – do not turn left or right.

4. Pass below a steep cliff face **(45 mins)** and, a few minutes later, pause to admire an old threshing circle on the left. From here, continue ahead and downhill.

    Pass through a pair of large iron gates **(1hr)** with a sign "Sóller a Pie" to the house called Ca'n Prohom. In the summertime, you should be able to buy freshly squeezed orange juice here. *Note – no allowance made for this orange juice stop – you may have to adjust timings from now on.*

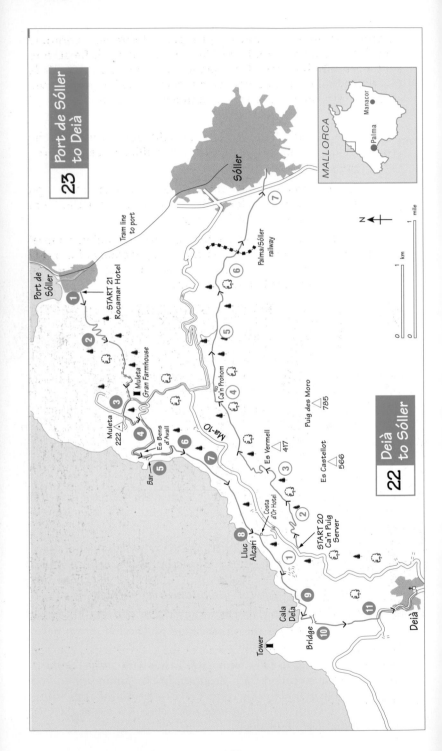

Suitably refreshed, or having just passed through, continue downhill to pass a dilapidated 13th-century chapel. Be sure to spot (**1hr 10mins**) the stone plaque on the right, "Camí de Castelló, rehabitat per l'escola de margers de Mallorca" – Consell Insula de Mallorca 1989. This commemorates the restoration of the track.

5. Pass a large restored building on your right. Soon, you'll see the mountain range behind Sóller – a truly magnificent scene – as the path continues past olive groves.

6. At a crossroads of paths (**1hr 25mins**), continue with a stone sign pointing reassuringly to Sóller. This is where you leave the Camí de Castelló and join the Camí des Rost.

    A few minutes later, cross above the Sóller-Palma railway line (if you're *really* lucky, you'll see the train. You get plenty of warning from its clanking and tooting as it makes its way around the wonderfully engineered mountain route).

A lucky view of the Sóller-Palma train

Continue along the stony track. This eventually becomes a tarmac road, leading past gardens and orange trees to the main road (the Sóller bypass).

7. Cross the main road, pass the petrol station (**1hr 45mins**) and

keep straight ahead – initially the church is in sight – until you reach Sóller's main square, Plaça de sa Constitució **(1hr 55mins).**

Other walks in the area

If you get back to Deià in plenty of time, there's an easy downhill 30-minute walk from the centre of the village to the small, horseshoe-shaped bay of Cala Deià. There are two routes: from Deià in the Valldemossa direction, turn right at the end of a wooden walkway opposite to a car park on the opposite side of the road and follow the side streets and then waymarks through olive groves to a tarmac road; in the Sóller direction, turn left at the GR221 sign and, follow the path down to the same tarmac road. In either case, turn left at the road and follow it down to the beach.

For a *very long* day, after arriving at Sóller take the tram to the port and follow the directions in Walk 23 to walk all the way back to Deià by the coastal route.

Places of interest

The busy village of **Deià** is worth exploring, either before your walk or when you can devote a morning at your leisure. Be warned: parking is becoming almost impossible, so get here very early (or leave it until late afternoon) or, better still, arrive by bus. Deià has acquired an upmarket reputation, reflected in soaring property prices and large numbers of aspiring artists and writers. The village has always attracted those of an artistic temperament; the most famous being the English poet and novelist Robert Graves. His daughter, Lucia Graves, continued the literary tradition with "A Woman Unknown", an account of her life in Mallorca and Spain. Her brother Robert wrote "Wild Olives", a frank description of their childhood.

Start your tour of Deià from the main road, near the cluster of shops. Walk uphill towards the church, following the Stations of The Cross (look for the ceramic wall plaques) to the highest point. Here you will find the church, next to which there is a small museum and the cemetery in which there is a simple headstone to Robert Graves (1895-1985), author of I, Claudius, The White Goddess and The Greek Myths. His house was opened as a museum in 2006.

Go behind the church and look out across the main road to the olive terraces – an impressive sight. Return to the village, where there are several craft shops, restaurants and a supermarket.

Along the road towards **Valldemosa**, be sure to call at **Son Marroig** – an interesting old mansion with attractive gardens. For details of both Valldemossa and Son Marroig, see Walk 26. Music lovers should note that an international music festival holds recitals at Son Marroig in the summer months.

23. Sóller/Port de Sóller to Deià
A coastal ramble

Grade: moderate

Distance: 15km

Time: 5 hours

Start: Platja d'en Repic, Port de Sóller

Finish: Deià village centre

How to get there: There are buses to the port or the tram from Sóller town. Note that the tram starts at the railway station and also picks up passengers at the bottom end of Plaça de la Constitució (the main square) just before the ice-cream shop. Get off the bus or tram at Sa Torre, this being the stop immediately before Repic beach.

If driving to the port on the Ma-11, do not go through the new tunnel. Instead, keep left to stay on the lower road and drive past the left turn for Platja d'en Repic and Faro Cap Gros. Continue to No Entry signs then turn left into the large car park at Sa Torre.

Map: IGN 670/II (1:25,000 – see reference chart in introduction)

Checklist: Walking boots; water; picnic; camera; bus times for return journey from Deià to Sóller

---

This links to the end of Walk 22 so you can either make a big day of it or tackle it in two halves, using any combination of transport. **Note: for map, see Walk 22.**

The Walk

From the car park, walk along a paved walkway to the Repic beach 'promenade'. Turn left, cross a bridge over the *Torrent* and you soon arrive at a telephone box and the Los Geranios hotel. Turn left here and keep walking along the road, passing the Campo-Sol restaurant. You soon pass the driveway to the dilapidated Rocamar hotel. It's anyone's guess as to how long it will remain standing, but it was still there at the end of 2008 after many years of neglect and decay.

1. Walk past the hotel building (15 mins) for 100m. Pass an information board and then turn right on the GR221 (signed to Deia and Muleta) up a steep cobbled path.

    Go through a steel gate to olive terraces (**25 mins**), with views of the bay opening up to the right. Continue through the terraces on a well-trodden path with occasional waymarks and cairns. Eventually, go up a series of steps, then through a gate and past a quarried area to the left.

Pause to admire the beautiful bay of the Port de Sóller

2. Continue climbing – but do pause, as if you need an excuse (**35 mins**) to admire the view of the bay. After a level section, another stepped path zig-zags upwards until, after a few more minutes, you are rewarded with the best view of all – see picture above! After another minute or so, you are on a more substantial track with reassuring signs to Deià and Muleta.

    Go through a gateway, over a streambed (**40min**) and then hard left on a cobbled path, soon with waymark signs for Deia and the Refugi de Muleta.

3. Go through a double gate and over a further streambed, following the GR221 signs around the Muleta complex, now restored.

    Walk along the main track to a T-junction, where you turn right (**1 hour**). Ignore the next junction and after just a few more minutes, you arrive at a tarmac road. From here, you can cut the walk short by turning left to meet the main Ma-10 and left again towards the Son Bleda hotel. From this point, choose from one of the following:

    a. Link up with the last section of the postman's path from Deià (see walk 20) by climbing the track opposite and following the waymarks to the Moli de San Mico – a large complex of buildings just off the main road; turn left on the main track from Deià and head to Sóller.

    b. Or, walk along the path to the left of Son Bleda and, after 100m, fork right at a sign to Sóller/Port de Sóller. Follow a waymarked track, securing all gates and ignoring a turn to the right. A 'Sóller and Port' sign appears and you eventually pass through double steel gates – someone will be itching to lock these. Pass signs for the GR221 to Refugi and Port de Sóller (Camí de Benidorm), neither of which are wanted, and keep straight on, passing the 19th-century Ca n'Ai hotel. At the main road follow the GR221 waymarks into Sóller.

c. As a final option: if you feel lucky, and really lazy, a bus may be on its way from Deià – the bus stop is just past the Son Bleda hotel!

4. **To continue the main walk**, turn right for 1.5km of a winding tarmac road down to Bens d'Avall restaurant. Follow the main tarmac road and ignore side turnings – an occasional "Restaurante" sign points you in the right direction.

   Eventually **(1hr 30min)** you approach the restaurant – where you *could* stop, but this is more a place for gourmets than hikers. So, about 50 metres before the building, at a large pine tree and a gap in the kerbstones, leave the road and cross a deep culvert using the iron pegs that have been hammered into the stone walls. This *really is* the correct route – there may be an easier way, but I have yet to find it!

Coastal erosion: a word of warning

The coastal path used in the next part of this walk is exposed in places and can be hazardous in wet weather. Mainly due to winter storms, the coast is subject to constant erosion and fallen trees are abundant so diversions are not uncommon. Also, there is a profusion of paths where walkers have found new routes around problem areas, and newer red dots and arrows often co-exist with older faded ones.

5. Warning noted, off we go – having crossed the culvert, turn right and walk along the lane towards the sea and behind the restaurant. After passing a house with a high retaining wall on your left, you come to a hairpin bend in the lane. Just before this bend, where a gutter ends on your left at a metal grid, turn left. A cairn just before a huge boulder marks the start of the path.

   This newer path is preferable to the narrower one a few metres below, even though the latter has red dot waymarks.

   Follow the (newer) red dots and cairns, go downhill to a terrace and down a short flight of stone steps. Turn left along a wide track with a drainage ditch on the left. Follow the red dots and cross a stile to the left of a double gate with a nearby Deià sign. Walk around a small gully **(1hr 45mins)**.

6. Go to the left of a ruined building then just to the right of a small shelter. Cross a stile and follow the path down to a lower level past

a series of cairns. In late 2008 fallen trees almost blocked the path, which also gets narrower until you reach a headland.

The path divides and it's best to fork left towards a more open area. Continue parallel to the sea then follow waymarks through a rocky area and up an awkward tree-strewn area to the remains of a stile.

7. Turn left uphill **(2hrs)** alongside a fence. The path then slants away from the fence and leads gently down to cross a large gully ('torrent'), which could be tricky in bad weather.

    Regain higher ground below olive terraces **(2hrs 15mins)**. The path goes through a broken terrace wall and then turns sharp left at the edge of pine woods along a narrow ridge, badly eroded seaward. At a clearing and the remains of an old watercourse, turn right (if, instead, you reach a metal gate, you have overshot by 20 metres).

    Follow waymarks to a path below the house on your left, then begin to walk away from the sea and up some steps. After the first few of these, fork right and keep parallel to the sea, still following the waymarks.

8. There's a larger house ahead **(2hrs 30mins)**. Keep to the right of it, below a large (and crumbling) upper retaining wall. Follow the path to a step-stile and a circular stone picnic table – albeit with a notice forbidding picnicking!

    To cut the walk short – or for refreshments – fork left and follow the winding track up through the woods, through the gateway marked 'Privado' which leads to the Costa d'Or hotel. There's an excellent bar and restaurant here – seasonal opening only. Afterwards, you can walk up to the Ma-10 to connect (eventually) with a bus, or return to the main route.

    To continue to Deià: from the stone table, continue in the same direction as before along a gently rising track. This soon joins a rock-edged path and crosses a couple of stiles. At a fork and a huge retaining wall, keep right (below the wall). At a gap in the pine trees, the path curves away to the right, away from the wall, and towards another circular stone table (you *can* picnic here!)

9. Follow steps down to a lower path **(3hrs)** and around the first part of an inlet. Soon you will be able to admire the rock formations worn away by the endless battering of the sea. How long before the most eroded one totters over?

    The path follows steps into the bottom of the inlet and climbs out again, soon passing a picnic area with a "take your rubbish home' request.

From here continue to a fork in the path and keep right, with the bay of Cala Deià below. Keep right at a second fork along a path edged by a rickety wooden fence. At a junction of paths, turn right to the beach and bars of Cala Deià where, at **3hrs 30mins**, we stop the clock for half an hour!

Cala Deià to Deià village

Suitably refreshed, (timing starts again from now) it's time for the final section. Head away from the beach along the main track to a tarmac road. You can relieve the tedium of road walking by spotting the stalactites in the mouth of the "cave" on your right, high up in a rocky outcrop.

10. After just a few minutes, turn right **(4hrs 20mins)** across the bridge, signed to Camí des Ribassos and go up a stepped track to a stile. Cross this and turn right to follow a track through an olive plantation. After 100m, turn a sharp hairpin left at a cairn – eyes peeled, as there are few waymarks. Deià is now straight ahead – so just keep walking along the attractive track until it widens and passes citrus plantations that are irrigated by the watercourse you eventually find on your right.

The bay of Cala Deià: a perfect place to laze in the sun

11. At **4hr 45min** you come to a road junction. Turn left at a "No Entry" sign and walk along a tarmac road then left again at a second "No Entry" – soon climbing steeply uphill. After a few minutes, you'll see a stepped alleyway ahead – take this up to the Ma-10 and turn left into the centre of Deià **(5hrs).**

To return to Sóller, you may find a convenient bus (about every two hours on a weekday, far fewer on a Sunday, so check current timetables.)

Other walks in the area

There are many walks in the Sóller and Deià areas, several of which are described in this book, but here is a short one that is worth trying:

Punta de Deià

My wife and I have often enjoyed the walk from Cala Deià to the old lookout tower at the end of the north-west headland, Punta de Deià. The tower was one of many lookouts dotted around the coast to pass on warnings of marauders, using smoke by day and fire by night.

A beautiful house and gardens now stand on the headland and, unlike some developments, the owners have provided a much-improved network of paths – so please respect their privacy.

There are two possible routes to the tower, and this is one of them: after a meal or a drink at the Ca's Patro March bar (the higher one, on the left of the beach) – walk through the bar itself (in the direction of the headland) to a zig-zag uphill path. Ignore the first path on the right, which leads to a house, and instead go up a stepped, overgrown path leading to a minor concrete road. Turn left and then, in 50 metres, turn right onto a tarmac lane. Follow the lane and you come to a sign telling you that it's "privado" straight ahead but that you can branch right to the lookout tower. Follow this path to the tower; there are wonderful views from here and beautiful flowers in springtime.

Return to Cala Deià by retracing your steps, or stay on the tarmac road to pass several other houses and go through a gate leading over a lane to the main access road to Cala Deià. (You can, of course, reverse this route to avoid going through the bar.)

Places of interest

Although this is the end of the walk itself, you should make time to visit the old village of Deià and especially the church with its wonderful views – see walk 22.

24. Sóller Lighthouse
An easy amble – with a twist in the tail

Grade: easy/moderate

Distance: 6km or 10km

Time: 1½ hours or 3 hours

Start & Finish: the Refugi de Muleta, above the port of Sóller

How to get there: drive up the steep and winding road from the port and park in the car park just beyond the lighthouse (*not* the private restaurant car park)

Map: maps are of no great help because the basic route is very simple, and the extension is not recorded on current maps

Checklist: walking boots; water; picnic; camera

From Faro Cap Gros – the lighthouse overlooking Port de Sóller – and the nearby Refugi de Muleta, you can enjoy an easy coastal stroll or add a little spice with a scramble up to the Muleta plateau. Either way, you soon leave casual strollers and are rewarded with sea views throughout most of your walk.

Faro Cap Gros – the lighthouse overlooking Port de Sóller

123

The Walk

1. Leave the car park, first following the GR221 sign for Sóller and Deià. After just a few metres, ignore the red/white marker and fork right along a wide track going gently downhill.

2. Keep to the left of a rocky headland until you reach an open area **(15 mins)** and a crossroads of paths. Go straight on and slightly downhill along a narrow, cairned track.

3. Eventually you're at the head of a small creek **(25 mins)**. From here, climb up and along a less-used route through shrubs and pampas grass. Small cairns and purple dots mark your way.

4. A few minutes later, you reach a junction with a rocky outcrop on your right. Turn left here, away from the sea, and continue uphill still following cairns. The route is straightforward with just one rocky stretch. Soon **(45 mins)**, you arrive at *Punta de Sóller*. There's a small, flat area near the top that's an excellent picnic spot – but keep well away from the edge and take extra care, especially with children, as there is a near-vertical drop from here.

   Look out to sea, across the bay of Port de Sóller, to the Picador tower, yet another of the ancient defensive towers around the coast of the island. Look a little more to the right and you can see Puig Mayor – the highest mountain on Mallorca, decorated with radar domes. To the left is Deià, and the rocky outcrop with a dip in the middle is Sa Foradada.

   Refreshed by the views, you now have a choice of routes:

   Either:

   Retrace your route, all the way to your starting point. Total time, about one and a half hours.

   Or:

   For the adventurous only, here is a diversion that takes you up to the Muleta plateau – this is a fabulous route but is fairly tough and should only be tackled by experienced walkers. *The timing for this section begins here.*

   From the top, scramble steeply down and in a generally north-easterly direction (towards Puig Mayor) following purple markers through a narrow gap in the rocks. After a couple of minutes, arrive at a small open area below a rock face; keep left here, with the sea ahead, and follow cairns and purple dots down to a broad valley.

5. Cross the valley and start climbing the cairned path on the opposite side **(15 mins)**. Note that it is **essential to follow the cairned (and purple-dotted) path**; if you have not seen a cairn or

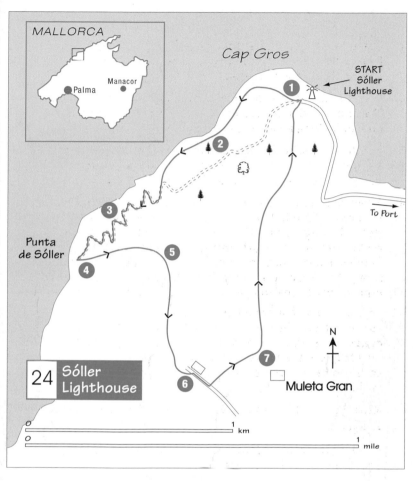

MALLORCA

Manacor
● Palma

Cap Gros

START
Sóller
Lighthouse

1

2

To Port

3

Punta
de Sóller

5

4

N

7

24 Sóller
Lighthouse

6

Muleta Gran

0 ———————————————— 1
km
0 ———————————————————— 1
mile

purple dot for 50 metres, turn back to the previous marked point
and try again – you have to be observant and look ahead!

The path bears slightly left (**25 mins**) with a rock face above and to
the right and later (**35 mins**) skirts another rock face, this time on
the left, before bending right. After another 10 minutes the path
heads uphill again through old terraces towards a dip in the
skyline.

Approaching the remains of a stone building (**40 mins**) fork left, to
a large cairn on a terrace wall. Turn right along the terrace, passing
the ruined building on your right and, very soon, a red-tiled
derelict barn.

*Just think: many years ago, people earned their living from this
inhospitable land. All of their supplies, and the crops they sold, had
to be carried by mule from and to the port.*

125

The Refugi – a welcome sight at the end of the walk

6. Continue along the cairned trail, now scarcely a path, until, eventually, you hit a wide gravel road (**1hr 10mins**) with a house 'Ca'n Tortuga' on the left. Walk along this road until you reach a main left turn, signed to the Refugi and the port (**1hr 20mins**).

Walk along the track and you soon will see the Muleta Gran complex over to your right. At a noticeboard and sign for the Refugi, turn left on a waymarked path. You soon pass through an arrowed gap in the wall and continue to the Refugi (**1hr 55mins**) and the car park.

The refuge was completed in 2006 and is very similar to that at Tossals Verds (see Walk 26) and Deià, offering basic food and refreshments plus accommodation, rather like a youth hostel. I wonder why we don't follow the Mallorcan example? In the UK, hostels could profit from catering for both hungry walkers and casual visitors. Book online here:
www.conselldemallorca.cat/mediambient/pedra/senderisme.php?opcio=20

Other Walks

There are many walks from Port de Sóller. Call into the Information Office for the local walks booklet. See also the next walk, over the La Muleta plateau.

25. Port de Sóller to La Muleta
The wide open plateau above Port de Sóller

Grade: moderate/strenuous

Distance: 10km

Time: 3 hours

Start & finish: Platja d'en Repic, Port de Sóller

How to get there: see walk 21

Map: IGN 670/II (1:25,000 – see reference chart in introduction)

Checklist: walking boots; water; picnic; camera

This is a walk with views of both the sea and rural Mallorca. A steep first half is followed by an easy amble across a high-level plateau and then a stroll to the Cap Gros lighthouse.

The Walk

The first part of this walk is identical to the first part of Walk 23 – so follow the instructions for that walk as far as point 3 which, suitably amended for this walk, is now changed to:

3. Go through a double gate and over a further streambed, following the GR221 signs around the complex. Walk along the main track – the GR221 sign now points to Refugi de Muleta and Deià – for just a couple of minutes to a signpost, pointing right to "Refugi" **(1 hour)**. Turn right here and follow the waymarked path.

Navigation across this section used to be difficult but the area has been cleared and the track is now obvious with waymarks along the way.

4. After about 10mins there is a potential straight-ahead short cut at a left-hand bend. We preferred to keep with the main path and, after 30mins, the GR221 is signed both ahead and to the left!

Go straight ahead – the refuge is just 5mins away. Follow this route and a pleasant surprise awaits.

This is far more than a 'refuge': it's a wonderful place for anyhting from a coffee to a meal – or even an overnight stay – see Walk 24.

5. Complete the walk by walking down the road to the port, which you should reach in about 30 minutes. There's no real alternative to this length of tarmac.

Other walks in the area

From the port it's an easy walk (or drive) to Sa Figuera with its orange groves (and orange juice!). Follow the signs from the centre of town. There are several other walks on the Muleta Gran – see Walks 23 and 24.

Places of interest

Port de Sóller has excellent beaches, plenty of bars and restaurants and, of course, the famous tram.

26. Font des Noguer to Tossals Verds
Water, Woods and Old Mallorca

Grade: moderate

Distance: 20km

Time: 5 to 6 hours

Start & Finish: the Font des Noguer car park

How to get there: Ma-10 from Sóller or Lluc. Limited parking above Cúber reservoir alongside the Ma-10, almost opposite the km34 marker post. There is a much larger car park at the Font des Noguer water supply and recreation area, just a few hundred metres down the Ma-10 in the direction of Lluc.

Maps: IGN 670/II & 671-1 (1:25,000 – see reference chart in introduction)

Checklist: walking boots; water; picnic; camera; emergency food supplies in case none available at the Tossals Verds mountain refuge

Notes: there are picnic tables and a Portakabin WC at the car park. Drinks and snacks are available at the Tossals Verds mountain refuge. For a full meal or accommodation, book ahead (Phone the refuge directly on 971 182027 or FODESMA – part of the Consell Insular – on 971 173638).

This is a walk with great flexibility. You can do the entire walk, include a mountain scramble, or just amble along and return when you've had enough. Whichever you choose, the route is very pleasant and is easy to follow, as most of the walk is within a park area that is now maintained by the Consell Insular de Mallorca – the island council – who have provided waymarks and are steadily improving facilities for walkers.

The Walk

1. From the car park, go down towards the main road and turn right to walk alongside a concrete watercourse – this connects Cúber to the nearby Gorg Blau reservoir via a pumping scheme. The track leads through a couple of gates with spring closures – but be sure that they do close, so that farm animals are kept away from the road.

    As the track bends to the right (**20 mins**) you get a wonderful view of Gorg Blau. This really blue stretch of water looks too good to be a reservoir, especially in spring time. Come in late summer, however, and it can be reduced to a pond.

2. Cross a bridge (**40 mins**) over the watercourse with a signpost pointing to Es Tossals Verds. Enter the park area and observe the

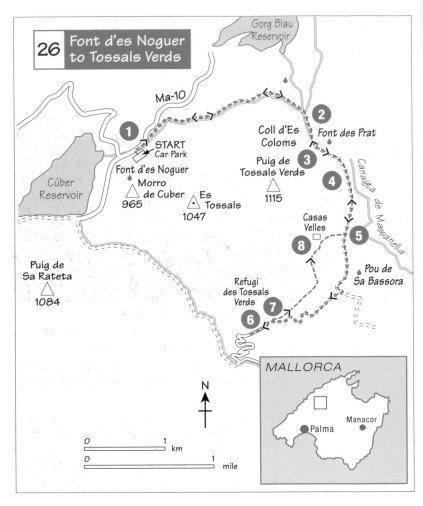

26 Font d'es Noguer to Tossals Verds

Gorg Blau Reservoir

Ma-10

START
Car Park

Coll d'Es Coloms

Font des Prat

Puig de Tossals Verds

Cúber Reservoir

Font d'es Noguer
Morro de Cuber
965

Es Tossals
1047

1115

Canaleta de Massanella

Casas Velles

Pou de Sa Bassora

Puig de Sa Rateta
1084

Refugi des Tossals Verds

MALLORCA

N

Manacor
Palma

0   1 km

0   1 mile

worrying "big game" sign. What are we supposed to do? Look out for bears? Wear a bullet-proof vest? Casting care to the winds, follow the stepped, stony path uphill through woodland.

As you climb, notice the flat circular areas alongside the path. These are the remains of *sitjas* – once fed by the vast plantations of holm oak (holly oak) that you see all around you. There are few remains of any other forms of agriculture (except for the farmstead that we see later in the walk) so charcoal must have been a valuable product.

You soon **(50 mins)** come to a sign pointing to the right, to the mountain of Puig des Tossals Verds, with an estimated 1 hour 15 minutes for the climb. If you can spare the 2-3 hours for the return

Gorg Blau, seen to perfection just after the start of the walk

trip, you'll be rewarded with splendid views. The time for this excursion is *not* included in the timing for this walk.

If you are not climbing the mountain (or are now returning from the ascent) continue downhill with a sign pointing to "Refugi des Tossals Verds".

3. After about ten minutes, you see a sign pointing to the left to "Font des Prat". It's only ten minutes each way to this spring, but I find it a bit disappointing. If you're really into springs, take a look – but there are more interesting diversions to come. Continue along the main path and, after another quarter of an hour, cross a bridge and keep following the signs to *Refugi*.

4. As the route levels out onto a clear stony track, look to the left and you should be able to see the arches of the "canaleta" – an old but well-engineered watercourse high on the face of the mountain. Further details of the canaleta are on page 138 of this book.

    Soon there are sweeping views of oak forests and then (**1hr 20mins**) to the left across a plain towards the town of Inca. In contrast to the woods surrounding us, there is a huge variety of agriculture in the *Pla* – the fertile valleys and plains of inland Mallorca.

5. After about ten minutes, you come to a more open area. In the spring there are masses of Asphodels, which die down in the summer to be replaced by the pink (and leafless) saffron-like flowers of the *Crocus cambessedessii*.

    Off the path, and to the left, is the impressive well of "Pou de Sa

Bassora". This is worth looking at – usually full of clear water and obviously of great importance in the past both to travellers and the farmers of this inhospitable landscape.

The nearest regular users of the well must have been the past inhabitants of the farmstead of Casas Velles de Tossals (the old houses of Tossals) just 5 minutes off to the right. Our return journey takes us to the remains of the farmhouse itself – but if you can't resist a peek right now, turn right at the signpost and pass a large threshing circle – evidence that this was once a very fertile area.

Continuing along the main track, pass a sign to 'Refugi (25 minutes)' and ignore the fork to Camí de Mancer (**1hr 50mins**). The woodland begins to change from oak to more recent conifers – while these are still young, you have a fine view of the L'Ofre mountain ahead and to the left.

Continue along the main track, ignoring any side tracks.

6. After two more signposts you arrive at the Refugi des Tossals Verds (**2hrs 15mins**).

   Although in a valley, the refuge is still at a height of 540 metres at the heart of the Serra de Tramuntana, within the Tossals Verds country estate. This was once a prosperous agricultural area, but was deserted by local people during the waves of emigration to which the region has been subjected over the past few hundred years.

Tossals Verds

The Refuge is a wonderful place for a break: modern, spotlessly clean WCs, a shelter, picnic tables and wonderful views. What more could you want? Well, if it's drinks and snacks, you've come to the right place. It also offers meals (take a chance but better to book ahead) and accommodation – shared dormitory and separate rooms. For accommodation, it's essential to book in advance. Go to: www.conselldemallorca.cat/mediambient/pedra/senderisme.php?opcio=20

The timing from here assumes a 30-minute break at the refuge.

For the return trip, head north-west from the refuge – i.e. with your back to the main building and the WC/shelter block on your left (**2hr 45mins**). Pass through a gate and climb a stony path for a few minutes before descending to follow a cliffside track, heading towards a valley – Coma de Tossals.

7. Continue walking along the floor of the valley and you soon pass an ancient well (**3hrs**). Before the arrival of piped water, wells would certainly have been needed around here. Contemplate that this wilderness once bordered onto fertile farmland – it's now more highly regarded for its spring flowers. Very soon you start to see the terraces below the Cases Velles (old houses) farmstead.

Only 50 years or so ago these terraces were still being cultivated on a small scale but, before that time, they provided a living in these harsh surroundings. The crops were mainly of olives, but there were also almonds and some cereals – recall the threshing circle that we saw earlier in the walk.

Eventually, the farms were abandoned. Mountain weather damaged the terraces and winter floods washed some of them away. However, thanks to a project funded by the European Union, work has started to restore the drystone walls (marjades) and eventually to replant traditional crops on the terraces. It will take a long time and considerable effort (and it would be nice if the explanatory FODESMA boards were in languages additional to Mallorquin – we're all paying for this!).

Climb onwards and upwards, out of the valley through ancient olives.

8. Soon **(3hr 35mins)** you're at the ruins of the Casas Velles farm-stead.

Have a look around – but be very careful, as the walls are in a poor state of repair. Inside one of the rooms, there are several circular stone blocks about two metres in diameter. Could they be grinding wheels for corn? Possibly – but I'm told that they were parts of olive presses. Either they were rotated against each other or rolled along a flat surface – the latter seems more likely, as there are no centre holes as in grinding wheels. Olives and olive oil were a staple part of the diet of these farming people, in addition to being a valuable crop.

From the main building, follow the wall for 50 metres and turn right through a large gap in the wall. Cross a water pipe and pass the threshing circle on your left. Very soon, you meet the main path **(3hr 50mins)** with the Basola well opposite – so turn left and retrace the remainder of the outward journey.

As things look different when walked in the opposite direction, here is a brief summary of what to look for:

Walk steadily uphill to a level section of path. Soon, it is time for a second view of the "canaleta" watercourse ahead and to the right.

The path descends to a bridge **(4hrs)** and you come to the signpost pointing left to Font des Noguer and right to Font des Prat.

In 1999, when these signs were new, other kind walkers had appended useful information such as "Cúber and Coll des Coloms" – both of which are useful landmarks.

After a quarter of an hour, you come to a sign pointing to Puig des Tossals Verds (left) and straight ahead to Font des Noguer. Continue on the stony track, pass the occasional *sitja* and go down the rough track and out of the park area. A backward glance at the sign tells you how lucky you were not to have been shot by big game hunters.

There's a bridge facing you. Cross the culvert (**4hr 30mins**) and turn left. Trudge back along the watercourse to the Font des Noguer car park (**5hr 15mins**).

If you parked at the Cúber car park, which is nearer to the Km34 marker post, cross the ladder stile and follow the footpath to avoid the Ma-10 .

Other walks in the area

There are several other splendid walks in the vicinity, including Puig de Massanella, best approached from the Ma-2130 road, about 1km south of Lluc. The *Mountains Tour & Trail Map* published by Discovery Walking Guides shows suitable routes. Puig Mayor is the biggest temptation, but you need either to go with an organised group or obtain a permit from the Spanish military authorities. UK residents should contact the Spanish Embassy in London; a possible route is described by June Parker in *Walking in Mallorca* (Cicerone Press). Finally, the adventurous route between Sa Calobra and Escorca along Es Torrent de Pareis is described in *Landscapes of Mallorca* (Valeri Crespi-Green).

Places of interest

Just a little further along the Ma-10 in the direction of Lluc is the twisting road down to Sa Calobra and its pretty beach. The monastery of Lluc is worth a visit. In both cases, get there early morning or late afternoon to avoid the crowds.

27. Cúber, Tunnels & Tossals Verds
A mountain adventure

Grade: strenuous

Distance: 13km

Time: 4½ hours (including a lunch break)

Start & finish: Cúber reservoir parking area (see below); if full, park at Font des Noguer (as used for Walk 24)

How to get there: see Walk 24

Map: IGN 670/II & 671/I (1:25,000 – see reference chart in introduction)

Checklist: walking boots; water; picnic; camera; torch *(essential – do not go on this walk without one)*; money – for a lunchtime drink and/or snack. You may also have to pay a fee of a euro or so to pass through one of the tunnels, though I've never had to do!

Notes: this is a "wild walk" through remote terrain: to reiterate from the "Checklist" section, you must take at least one torch on this walk to guide you and your party through the tunnels. You should be able to buy snacks at the half-way point, the Refugi Tossals Verds, but be sure to take emergency rations just in case! See Walk 24 for details of the Refuge.

Here's a walk for those of you who love an adventure. It's set in one of the wildest parts of Mallorca, yet you're likely to meet quite a few walkers – mostly at the beginning and middle of the walk. A major feature is Cúber reservoir – El Embalse de Cúber – one of the main water-catchment areas for this part of the island, the other being Gorg Blau, north-east of Cúber. The two are connected by a watercourse, but water is also piped south-west towards Lloseta and – fortunately for us – the water board engineers constructed tunnels up to 150 metres in length to take their supply pipes across the mountain by the shortest possible path. These tunnels are used on our walk.

Moving uphill – towards Font des Noguer and the Ma-10 – there are huge forests of holm oak (holly oak; *Quercus Ilex*). This was the best sort of wood for charcoal production – and we will see evidence of this traditional Mallorcan rural industry on our walk.

There is a choice of two routes back from the refuge to your starting point. Both lead, ultimately, to the modern watercourse connecting Gorg Blau to Cúber. Along the way, whichever route you choose, you pass near to a derelict farmhouse, ancient but still functioning wells, and an intriguing old aqueduct. If that isn't enough, there's also the prospect – for the extremely energetic – of a side-trip up a nearby mountain.

The Walk

If you had to park at Font des Noguer, walk uphill (Sóller direction) to the small car park for Cúber reservoir (almost opposite the km34 marker post on the Ma-10). There is no need to walk along the busy road – use the ladder stile leading from the car park and walk along the path instead.

1. From the start point, go through the gate and head roughly south-west towards Cúber reservoir. Walk along the track until you reach a concrete blockhouse just before the dam wall **(10 mins)**.

    As you walk down to the reservoir Puig de sa Ruteta is ahead and Moro de Cúber is to the left. The highest mountain in Mallorca, Puig Mayor (1443m) is behind you – though you can't see the summit from here.

2. Turn left before the dam and go downhill along a rough track. Ignore a right fork – just keep on the higher, main track. As the path steepens, take care on the loose scree.

    Soon **(20 mins)**, you come to a large concrete pipe on your left which you *must* ignore – this is *not* one of the tunnels used on this walk. Just keep going down the steep, stony track.

3. At the foot of the ravine, cross the streambed **(25 mins)**. Most of the time this will be dry – but if it is in flood, don't take chances – you may have to return from this point.

    Just a few metres after crossing the streambed, turn left at a T-junction with a concrete wall on your right.

    Continue down the rough, stony, pampas-overgrown track. Beware of the additional hazard of spiky brambles dangling down-wards from the branches. After a cautious descent, you meet your first tunnel **(45 mins)**.

4. Torches on – it's time to walk through a mountain! Walk carefully for about 100 metres to the end of the unlit tunnel.

    After about 200 metres in the open, you meet your second tunnel, diving off into the cliff on your right. No daylight is visible from the other end at first – and there's about 150 metres of tunnel to walk through this time!

    At the end of this tunnel, turn right at the pumping station and a rusting cement mixer. Keep a lookout for the gorse-like streamers that are just waiting to scratch your face.

    Continue downhill with another concrete wall for company (these seem to be here to protect the water pipes).

    The next tunnel (number 3) is preceded by a "Private Property' sign with the threat of a fee to pass through. Be prepared.

Cúber reservoir: the start of our adventure!

About 200 metres after emerging from this lengthy tunnel, you pass through tunnel number four – a very short one this time, more of a rock arch – before passing through the final tunnel. At the end of this one, you turn right at a brick-built blockhouse.

Go down a wide track and ignore any red arrows pointing off the main route.

5. The winding trail continues down the valley until you reach an intersection **(1hr 20mins)**. Ignore the right fork – keep to the left, marked by a small cairn.

    After a few minutes, you reach some steel gates on your left. Cross the steel ladder stile to the left of the gate and, after 50 metres, turn left up a concrete road.

    Continue along this road to some steps on the right **(1hr 35mins)** and a sign telling you that it's only 10 minutes to the refuge. Follow this path up through the olive groves. Towards the end, it becomes well paved and soon it meets a road where you turn right. There's a sign here pointing back (the way you've just walked) to Lloseta, Alaró and Orient.

6. After just a few minutes, you enter the grounds of the Refugi Tossals Verds.

    Before you use the facilities or the restaurant, take a stroll around the gardens, which include traditional Mallorcan crops. The refuge lies within a recreational area that is a great credit to the Island Council of Mallorca — routes are waymarked, tracks are being improved and visitors are encouraged.

Timings from this point assume a 30-minute break.

Suitably refreshed, walk behind the main building, up some stone steps, past a couple of olive trees and through a gate (**2hrs 20mins**).

Note: this route takes you on the *higher* path, above the valley. There is an alternative route through the Sa Coma agricultural area, described in Walk 24. Just be sure that you are following this higher route if that is your intention — the lower route goes above and behind the toilet block.

7. Climbing uphill, you soon fork right at the a sign to "Font des Noguer 1hr 50 min". Continue uphill, but take a breather to look down on the old terraces, which are being restored (**2hrs 45minutes**).

    Keep your eyes open and, after a few minutes you'll see, up on the left, the remains of Casas Velles ("old houses") with the mountains of Tossals Verds behind. We visit the houses later.

8   Eventually (**3hrs**) the path levels out to a wide plain. In the spring, there are asphodels and, in the autumn, purple-flowering colchicums brighten the landscape.

    On the right, a path leads to the ancient well of "Pou de Sa Basola"; return to the main path after your visit.

    This impressive, deep well is usually full of clear water (though I'm distrustful of drinking from any well). It's all the more remarkable for being set so high up, remote and distant from other water sources.

    On the left, you can follow the sign from the main track to the even more fascinating Casas Velles de Tossals — the old houses.

    On the way to the houses, notice the threshing circle on the right, suggesting that cereal crops were almost certainly grown here. See Walk 24 for a description.

    Return from the house and continue along the main track, soon overlooking a heavily wooded valley.

    You are walking amongst holm oak trees (*quercus ilex*) — much favoured for charcoal production.

9. After a few minutes, just as the path starts to climb, look up and right and you'll see a superb arched, stone aqueduct set in the mountain side.

    This is the Canaleta de Massanella, a famous aqueduct that was used to take water from the Font des Prat (see below) to the farms and houses of Massanella. According to Valeri Crespi Green in "Landscapes of Mallorca" (published by Sunflower Books) this was

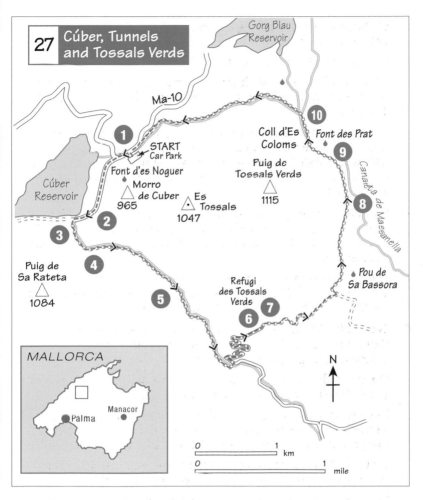

designed and built by a local pig farmer after professional engineers had pronounced it to be an impossible task.

Cross a stream, then re-cross it via a bridge. Soon, go up some steps to continue a gentle uphill climb.

Around here you should see your first sitja, recognisable as a flat, circular area (2hrs 30mins).

After a few minutes, there's a sign on the right to Font des Prat – a nice enough picnic spot, but only worth the diversion if you are interested in Mallorcan wells.

Continue uphill – there's a reassuring sign pointing ahead to "Font des Noguer, 1hr" – though it would be better if the more familiar Ma-10 were included. There's also a sign pointing left to "Puig de

Tossals Verds, 1hr 15 minutes" – but unless you have a huge surplus of energy, come back another day!

Continue along the track, which soon heads downhill, passing another *sitja*, and leaving the park area.

10. Cross a bridge **(3hrs 45mins)** and turn left to follow the concrete watercourse all the way back to the Font des Noguer recreation area **(4hrs 15mins)**.

I've often reflected on how nice it would be to take a canoe along the watercourse. Font des Noguer is one of the places where locals replenish their containers with spring water – so you need have no qualms about drinking from here!

11. By now you are either back at your car (at Font des Noguer) or just 10 minutes away from the Cúber reservoir starting point. A lengthy, but enjoyable walk – with the prospect of telling everybody how you walked through a mountain!

Other walks and places of interest
See Walk 26.

28. Valldemossa, Teix and the Archduke's Walk

Travels without a Donkey

Grade: Strenuous

Distance: 14km

Time: 6 -7hrs

Start & Finish: Valldemossa town centre

How to get there: Valldemossa is on the Ma-1130 road, about 2km from its intersection with the Ma-10 . There are plenty of buses.

Map: IGN 670/II & 670/IV (1:25,000 — see reference chart in introduction)

Checklist: Walking boots; water; picnic; camera

Luckily for us, the Archduke Ludwig Salvador became quite overweight whilst in Mallorca. To enable him to continue to enjoy the delights of his Valldemossa estate, he ordered the construction of a series of paved pathways, so that he could be conveyed on horseback between his favourite viewpoints *(miradors)*. This quirk of fate provides us with a high mountain route – the famed Camí d'Arxiduc.

We also have the option – not compulsory, but well worth considering – of a climb up to the top of Teix (1064m). This rocky mountain rewards you with views of the whole of Mallorca's north and west from one lofty vantage-point.

As you can see from the sketch map for this walk, our route is in an anticlockwise direction. Naturally, you can complete the walk clockwise via Es Pouet, Caragoli and Teix but this means that you'll be tired by the time you get to the foot of Teix and less inclined to climb it. Also by the time you get there the weather is more likely to have changed – even in the summer. As a final argument, the beginning of the walk is easier to describe when tackling it in this direction!

The Walk

1. Start from either of the main car parks in Valldemossa and walk up the Ma-1130 in the Palma direction. Turn right at the first corner and you see a big, old building with a square tower. Go straight on, past this building with a "Luis Vives" sign. At a T-junction, turn right along Carrer Toscano and you soon pass a huge, pillared gateway. This is where you leave the housing development of Valldemossa.

2. Fork left **(20 mins)** along a wide track with an old iron gate and a sign to "Refugi" – this really is just a mountain refuge, unlike the splendid hostels of Tossals Verds, Ca'n Boi and La Muleta. Follow

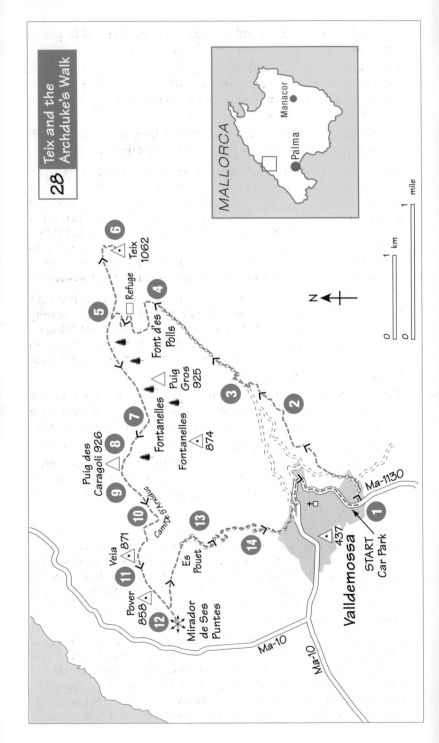

28 Teix and the Archduke's Walk

MALLORCA

Manacor

Palma

N

0 1 km

0 1 mile

Teix 1062

6

Refuge

5

4

Font d'es Polls

Puig Gros 925

3

2

Fontanelles

7

Fontanelles 874

Puig des Caragoli 926

8

9

Camí de s'Arxiduc

10

Veia 871

11

Pover 858

12

13

Es Pouet

14

Mirador de Ses Puntes

Ma-1130

Valldemossa

437

START Car Park

1

Ma-10

Ma-10

the main track as it meanders along, ignoring any side paths. There are excellent views into the fertile valley to your right.

Go over a cattle grid **(35 mins)** and through a gateway to a T-junction, where you turn left again with a "Refugi" sign to point you upwards. As you toil up the track, an exhilarating view of the Teix massif begins to open up ahead.

A few minutes later, there is another T-junction, possibly still without a sign. Turn right here – do *not* go straight ahead.

3. You next come to the large wooden gates **(45 mins)** forming the entrance to the Son Moragues recreational park – an area administered by the Consell Insular de Mallorca – the Island Council of Mallorca. Cross a large step stile along the gates and walk uphill past the FODESMA-administered area. After a few minutes you can make a diversion to see the remains and constructions of some of the old Mallorcan rural industries, such as charcoal burning, limestone ovens and the netting of thrushes.

4. Pass the Font des Polls spring and note, *but don't take*, the right turn to Serra d'es Cairats **(1hr 5mins)**. Instead, continue steadily uphill. Just 10 minutes later, you arrive at the mountain refuge – always with the lingering smell of wood smoke; there are no toilets or catering facilities here, but it does provide shelter for those intent on backpacking expeditions.

The main track continues from the refuge – at first along the flat and then up a tougher and rockier uphill zig-zag. After a little more climbing the path levels out again and comes to a large cairn.

5. Turn right at the cairn **(1hr 40mins)** and you'll find yourself some 100 metres away from a small group of pines. **Decision time** – those not going to Teix can wander along to the pines and shelter from the sun while the hardier members go for their optional mountain excursion.

6. If there's no sunshine, there's no real point in going up Teix – so let's assume it's a clear, sunny Mallorcan day and that Teix is our next destination. Walk to the right, in the general direction of the mountain, noting the proud notice declaring it to be the property of the state. Cross a wall, go down an iron ladder at the other side and continue onwards and upwards until you reach the top, marked with a concrete pillar.

It takes 30 minutes to climb Teix and almost the same time to get back to the pines. From the top you'll look north to Puig Mayor the highest mountain in Mallorca (but out of bounds because it's a military communications site, though you can apply for permission to climb to the top – good luck: it's a tough walk!) Galatzó is to the west and the bay of Palma to the south.

After the climb to Teix, you arrive back at the pine trees (**2hr 40mins**). Take a break from your exertions.

The timing on this walk assumes that you reward yourself with 30 minutes of relaxation here.

Continue from the pines in a westerly direction along the stony Camí d'Arxiduc.

7. You now come to a much larger group of pines, an area called "Fontanelles" (**3hr 40min** – remember that half hour in direction 6!). From here a path heads off at 45° to the left for anyone who wants to shorten the walk. It leads to the old spring of Es Pouet (see later).

8. Continue along the path and, after 15 minutes or so, you come to the small peak of Puig de Caragoli (944m). Make the small ascent of 20-30 metres from the track and you'll be rewarded with a fine view and a plaque erected by the mountaineers of Mallorca in gratitude to the Archduke.

   At the top of the next rise (**4hrs**) there is a cairned path leading off to the right. It goes steeply down to Deià (near to the Es Moli hotel) – this path is not followed on our route but it could be useful for a quick descent in bad weather.

9. From this point along the Archduke's trail there are spectacular views to the right, particularly of the rocky headland of Sa Foradada ('the pierced one') near to Son Marroig, to compensate for the rough going under foot and vertigo-inducing cliffs just a few feet away. In poor weather, stay away from the edge!

10. After going over one final rocky hump (**4hr 20mins**) with more wonderful views, the path drops into a wooded area. Follow the main rock-edged path. After a few minutes, turn right through a prominent gap in the rock-edged path, marked by a red dot and the word DEIA behind the rocks.

    Go through a gap in a stone wall (**4hr 40mins**) and then continue down a rocky path. You now come to a stone bench. For another short cut to Es Pouet, turn left here. Otherwise, go straight ahead and uphill, following the red dots. At the top of the hill, you come to a ruined shelter – which would be much more useful if the Island Council invested in a roof.

11. Continue from the shelter along a level, waymarked track to the headland and soon you will again be walking along the Camí d'Arxiduc. A square-pillared triangulation point is the next feature along the walk (**5hr 5mins**), and from here our destination is the famed Mirador de ses Puntes – the Archduke's favourite viewpoint. The path curves downhill and to the left. Going downhill to the mirador might seem unlikely – but believe me, it is

Diana on The Archduke's Bridleway

correct. Save yourself a few moments by taking a short cut (waymarked) across a flattish stony area. The route soon levels out to another rock-edged path.

12. At a hairpin bend in the path **(5hr 20mins)**, you can look out (take care – steep drop here) before continuing downhill for about 70 metres where, finally you turn right along a track marked with small cairns) to the famous Mirador. Walk back along the track from the Mirador for just 20 metres and fork right along a stony downhill track.

13. After a few minutes, the path enters a clearing with, in the centre, the old well of Es Pouet ("Pou" in Mallorquin is the word for "well", and Pouet is "little well"). Walk straight across the clearing, past the Es Pouet well **(5hr 50mins)** and continue the downhill walk – slowed by the rough conditions underfoot. After about 20 minutes of this, cross the stile and, just a couple of minutes later, turn right onto a smooth, wide gravel track. This soon becomes the tarmac surfaced road of Carrer de los Oliveres.

15. Continue downhill and, just before the football pitch (on your right), turn left along another road that leads directly to the lower of the two car parks on the Ma-1130 after a total of nearly six and a half hours. Time for a refreshing cool drink!

Other walks in the area

You can also arrange to visit the island of Sa Foradada – tickets available from Son Marroig.

Places of interest

The town of **Valldemossa** is very popular, especially in the mornings when coachloads of visitors arrive for the mid-morning concerts. The big attraction is the Real Cartuja – the Carthusian church and monastery dating from the 15th century. The "Real" means "royal" and refers to the Palace of King Sancho, which preceded the monastery which, in turn, became a secular property in 1835.

Chopin, accompanied by his mistress George Sand, stayed here in the winter of 1838. "George" was a divorcee, born Aurore Duplin; she thought the island climate would improve Chopin's health, but the uncharacteristically dismal winter weather only made it worse. She went on to write "A Winter in Mallorca", which was critical of the local people. Two pianos used by Chopin can be seen in the museum.

The Archduke Ludwig Salvador of Austria was the other well-known local resident. Always the black sheep of the Austrian royal court, the wealthy archduke had an eye for the ladies and was frequently the target of wagging tongues – especially concerning his alleged romantic entanglements with Sisi, the Empress of Austria. He bought the **Son Marroig** estate between Deià and Valldemossa and eventually owned many more estates all over the island. The Son Marroig mansion, originally a monastery, is just a few kilometres from Valldemossa on the road to Deià. The house is packed with paintings and memorabilia and is also the venue for a series of classical concerts. I recommend these – in the concert interval, you can watch the sun set while sipping a chilled *fino*; what could be more romantic?

Ludwig's greatest achievement was to record the natural history, rural life and folklore of the Balearics in his illustrated "Die Balearen Geschildert in Wort und Bild" published in 1897. There are several other editions, including a handsome limited edition in Spanish, with the title "Las Baleares".

29. Sóller, Es Cornadors & Alfàbia
The Pilgrim's Path plus a mountain adventure

Grade: strenuous

Distance: 12km (there and back) or 17km

Time: 5 hours or 7 hours

Start & Finish: Biniaraix, at the Sóller end of Carrer de Ozones, approximately 1km north-east of Sóller town centre. Please do not park in the centre of Biniaraix, as it is a very small village with narrow streets.

How to get there: Follow the signs from Sóller to Biniaraix and park on the approach road to Biniaraix. Buses to Sóller from all parts of the island, train from Palma or tram from Port de Sóller. On foot, it is about 1km from the centre of Sóller to the start of the walk.

Map: IGN 670/II & 670/IV (1:25,000 – see reference chart in introduction)

Checklist: walking boots; water; picnic; camera

This walk takes you from the pretty village of Biniaraix, just outside Sóller, along Es Barranc – the famous pilgrims' path. Having got to the top, you can continue over all the way to Lluc or return to Sóller. What you cannot easily do is a circular route with a return through the S'Arrom estate; this was the traditional route until a few years ago, when the landowners prohibited access except to local guides who pay for access. You may be able to find a contact with a key by asking at your hotel or tourist information centre. An alternative excursion is described across the wild and rugged Alfàbia ridge.

The Walk

1. From the three ornate crosses at the Sóller end of Carrer d'Ozones, follow the sign for Biniaraix. After a few minutes, turn left over a bridge and continue towards the village, pausing to admire the Alfàbia ridge, up on the right. At a phone box (**15 mins**) go up a series of cobbled steps and continue up Carrer de Sant Guillem to the tiny village square, Plaça de la Concepció.

    For a nice start to the day, have a fresh orange juice in the shop-cum-bar on the right-hand side of the square.

2. Leave the square along Carrer de Sant Josep, following the old sign (or maybe a new one by now!) indicating "Lluc a pie". A few minutes later, turn right at the wash-house along a wide gravel track. After a few more minutes, fork right along a cobbled track that eventually leads to the stone steps of es barranc (the ravine). This is the way the pilgrims came on their way to the monastery at Lluc.

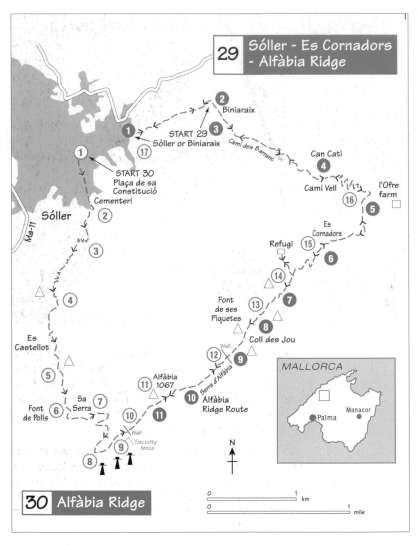

29 Sóller - Es Cornadors - Alfàbia Ridge

Biniaraix

START 29
Sóller or Biniaraix

Cami des Barranc

Can Cati

START 30
Plaça de sa
Constitució

Cami Vell

l'Ofre
farm

Cementeri

Sóller

Es
Cornadors

Refugi

Font
de ses
Piquetes

Es
Castellot

Coll des Jou

MALLORCA

Alfàbia
1067

Serra d'Alfàbia

Alfàbia
Ridge Route

Sa
Serra

Font
de Polls

Manacor

Palma

Wall

Security
fence

N

30 Alfàbia Ridge

0   1
                    km
0   1
                              mile

3. After crossing a bridge, the route is uphill all the way. Cross a second bridge **(40 mins)** and, five minutes later, you come to some ruins; keep left here and continue uphill. Very soon you pass alongside piping that will accompany you for much of the way.

    Have a breather along here and look back to Sóller. A little further along, look at the rock formations on your right – can you see the dog's head and a pair of legs?

4. Pass some summer dwellings **(1hr)**. The path levels out, but not for long. Keep straight on, following the track.

5. The track continues remorselessly uphill – but do stop from time

Diana pausing for breath on Es Barranc

to time, if only to admire the view! Go through some steel gates **(1hr 40mins)** and along a level track until you come to a signpost **(2hrs)** pointing across a bridge to "Mirador de'n Quesada & Es Cornadors". Cross the bridge into part of the L'Ofre estate and an open area with a few shady trees that are ideal for a lunch break – *the timing from here allows for a 15-minute break.*

6. Start again **(2hrs 15mins)** up a stony track and head towards the "horns" of the Es Cornadors pass; look back towards the large and impressive L'Ofre farm and the mountains beyond, including L'Ofre (1098m). Continue up a zig-zag donkey path until the ground levels out **(2hrs 50mins)** and you will soon find a concrete sign pointing to the mirador.

    Just a little way up the hill there is a shelter – handy for a later lunch stop – and you can also continue over to the mirador.

Options

From here, you used to be able to return via the S'Arrom estate: facing downhill, with your back to the shelter, the route goes off to the right (from the concrete sign we passed earlier) and over the wall, where there used to be a stile. This route is no longer passable unless you are prepared for some very awkward climbing around locked gates or you happen to have a key to open the padlocks. Other choices are:

A: return directly to Sóller: this will take about 2 hours without a break. The scenery will look very different in the opposite direction and you will have more time to admire the views now that you are not toiling up a steep hill. If you need directions, refer to points 17 onwards in Walk 30.

B: Proceed to the Alfàbia summit. The instructions provided here are for a there-and-back trip to the summit, following which you return to Sóller down the barranc, as in option A.

C: Circular route via Alfabia. If you feel really adventurous, you can extend the walk beyond the Alfàbia summit towards the radio masts and back to Sóller.

The Alfàbia Summit

This route is only for experienced walkers – navigation is not easy and, because of nearby steep cliffs, it should not be attempted in bad weather.

7. Walk downhill from the shelter, cross the pass and start walking uphill to a group of trees. At first the path is clear, but it soon grows fainter, though there are cairns to mark your route all the way up to the ridge. Pass just to the right of the first peak – i.e. follow the cairns to begin with, but ignore the one at the highest point.

8. Follow the limestone plateau round to the right, heading south-west to the distant radio masts – these appear and disappear as you walk along the ridge. A spectacular near-vertical cliff drops away to your right – just keep about 20 metres away from the edge as you continue across this splendid isolated landscape.

    Again: heed my warning – if the weather is other than excellent, turn back – there are no marks awarded for bravery! If the weather is good, carry on but take your time on the uneven surface.

9. Eventually **(3hrs 30mins)** you reach a wall; cross it near to a metal sign and bear right through a very rough area of rocks and pampas.

    On your left, there are good views of Cúber reservoir and Puig Mayor.

10. Keep left of the next major rock outcrop **(3hrs 45mins)** and walk across an area of "limestone pavement" – a landscape feature of huge cracks and apparent blocks of limestone caused by weathering and erosion.

    A few holly oaks dot the plateau, but ahead you should still be able to see the aerials.

    At the end of the plateau, descend through a small wooded area and a wall will be seen on the right-hand side. Continue uphill and parallel to the wall. At the top of this hill, the wall bends to the left. Cross the wall where it has been trodden down, then bear right for an extraordinary view of Sóller, with the port in the far distance.

11. Continue parallel to the cliff edge. After a few more minutes **(4hrs**

20mins) a new peak faces you. This leads up to the summit of Alfàbia (1068m) topped by a white marker post.

Return to Sóller by following the instructions from number 12 in walk (28). It will take about 3hrs 30mins – quite a long day!

Circular route

Follow the previous section to the summit of Alfàbia. Continue beyond the summit on a path that descends to a wide track. After about 200 metres, you have a choice:

If you don't mind taking a gamble, go through the wide gateway to the left of the fence and walk along the well-surfaced track. Keep an eye on the outcrop to the right and, when you see it drop into a dip just before a further outcrop immediately before a radio mast, find a gap in the security fence and head sharply right, to the dip that you spotted.

or

If you don't fancy the above, keep to the right of the fence and clamber through the pampas grass and over rocks for 30-40 min, keeping near to the fence until you see a gap on the far right, before the antennae. Cross a broken wall and continue ahead with the wire-mesh security fence on your left. Terrain permitting, head to the right and find the dip in the rocks on the right before the antennae.

From this dip, by whichever way you reached it, cross a low wire fence on your right, and scramble down to a track which zig-zags down to a wide, level track. Turn left along this, continue for about 150 metres then turn right to pass the Sa Serra farm building. With your back to the antennae, head diagonally to the right along a waymarked track (red dots) to a cairn. Go left here and then, after 50 metres, turn right towards a larger cairn.

From here, red waymarks take you downhill in the direction of Sóller. After about an hour and a half, you should see the sign for the Sóller boundary (two lions beneath a radiant sun). Continue down to olive groves, turn right and emerge on a road. Turn right and walk past the cemetery down to the centre of town.

Other walks and places of interest

See Walk 30.

30. The Alfàbia Ridge
An anti-clockwise adventure

Grade: strenuous – very!

Distance: 15 extremely long kilometres

Time: 9 hours

Start & Finish: see Walk 27

How to get there: see Walk 27

Map: IGN 670/II & 670/IV (1:25,000 – see reference chart in introduction)

Checklist: walking boots, camera, plenty of liquid and food. Mountain walking gear appropriate for the season. Mobile phone may be useful.

Notes: It is not advisable to attempt this walk on your own. In the unlikely event of an accident, a competent companion will be greatly appreciated!

This is a tough walk and you may wonder why it should be attempted, but there are two good reasons: firstly, it provides a circular walk based, in part, on the 'pilgrim' route from Biniaraix to Es Cornadors now that the S'Arrom estate has been gated off and, secondly, it's a great challenge along a wild, remote ridge with incredible views.

Be warned: though cairned in places, most of the ridge is pathless with exposed, awkward limestone. It is not well walked and you are unlikely to meet anybody so – to repeat my warnings in Walk 29 – do not attempt this walk alone. If you slip, twist your ankle, or worse, the likelihood of rescue is very remote. You have been warned!

Why anti-clockwise? Why not just continue the clockwise route in the previous walk? Simply because the anti-clockwise route is easier to follow and to describe. One final warning – if you do attempt this route in a clockwise manner, i.e. simply by reversing these instructions, I feel that it is inadvisable to attempt a descent from the ridge other than the reverse of the ascent described. The tempting track to the east of the Alfàbia peak leads into private property and locked gates while the descent west of Alfàbia is badly eroded and potentially dangerous.

Note: for map, see Walk 29.

The Walk

Start the walk from the Plaça de sa Constitució in the centre of Sóller. There are several nice pastry shops where you can stock up with provisions for the day ahead.

1. Walk along the road (Carrer J. Bapta ensenyat) to the left of the church then left onto Carrer Santa Barbara and right into Sant Nicolau. Go left, then immediately right onto Carrer de Pablo Noguera and walk all the way up to the municipal cemetery. This is not an omen.

2. Walk uphill from the cemetery. Follow the road round to the right, ignoring the track straight ahead. After about 200 metres, go left up stone steps, marked with a red dot. (There is an overgrown path across the road, continuing down to Sóller.)

3. Follow a waymarked path through olive groves. This path is clear and well waymarked. Where it levels out **(35 mins)**, keep to the left. Follow the red dots – sprayed at regular intervals onto rocks – along a stepped path until you cross a Sóller town border sign (two lions beneath a sun).

    Note: the red dots (waymarks) are very carefully done and there is never more than a 25-metre gap between them. If you run out of dots, go back immediately to your last point of reference, or you will definitely get lost!

4. Go through a gate **(1hr 30mins)**, across a grassy area and continue uphill. Pass below a peak on your right and eventually **(2hrs 30mins)** you have your first sight of the antennae on the ridge ahead – you are now at a height of about 710m.

5. Keep below and to the left of a further small peak. Take a 10-minute break – look down the valley and you can see Puig Mayor – the highest mountain in Mallorca.

    Restart your walk, heading for the distant masts and following – very carefully – the red waymarks.

6. Emerge at a large cairn **(3hrs)** on a plateau with the ridge facing you – dots mark your path between the rocks. After 10 minutes, you come to a flat grassy area. Turn left at a small cairn, then right towards the Sa Serra farm building. From here, there are no more red dots! Walk towards a fence and follow it to hit a wide track leading from the building. Turn left along this track.

7. Ignore the track heading left after about 50 metres. After a further 100 metres, turn right off the main track, up a one-time vehicle track which zig-zags in the general direction of the antennae. After a few minutes, the track dips downhill and, at **3hrs 45mins**,

it rounds a large reinforced hole in the ground. Head uphill from here towards a prominent wind turbine until a higher path is reached, which leads to a solitary tree no more than 50 metres below the col (the dip on the ridge – the lowest point between the antennae and the main ridge).

8. Walk up from the tree and zig-zag up to the end of the fence (**3hrs 50mins**). Either continue up to a plain (i.e. not barbed) wire fence and climb over it or scramble slightly to the left – in either case, gaining the col. Turn left and walk up to the ridge.

   NOTE: this next section is difficult and hard going. There is no path, no waymarks and few cairns to guide you.

9. Choose the easiest route between the ridge on your left and the security fence below you. Eventually (**4hrs 40mins**) you reach the corner of the security fence. Scramble past a holly oak tree that partially obstructs your path and climb over a broken wall.

   Note that you may find a convenient gap in the wire fence; if so, go through it and turn left for about 500m to a gateway. See 'Circular Route' notes for Walk 29.

10. From the end of the fence (or, if you found a gap in the fence, on passing through the wide gateway) go along a wide track for about 200 metres then fork right up a stony path. After a few minutes, the distinctive white marker post (some 2 metres high) on top of the Alfàbia peak comes into view. Although the cairned route skirts to the right of the peak, it's an easy scramble to the top for a well-earned break with magnificent views in all directions.

Made it! The author with walking chum Brian, celebrating on top of Alfàbia.

Continue from Alfàbia (**5hrs 15mins**) – follow the cairns, going left into a hollow and following more cairns along a faint track with a limestone cliff away up to your right.

11. Now head up to a small peak (**5hrs 30mins**). Cross the peak and head to the right-hand side to pick up the track again. Go downhill to a couple of holly oaks, a cairn and a grassy stretch. Follow occasional cairns, keeping close to the Sóller side of the ridge.

12. Cross a wall to a cairn straight ahead. Bear left and keep parallel to the wall, 50 metres on the left. Bear right and pass between two cairns to an area of holly oaks. Continue with the wall still 30 metres or so on the left – don't be tempted by a row of cairns heading to the right: your way is straight ahead. When the wall ends, head for a cairn on the skyline.

    You are now in an amazing area of classic "limestone pavement" – deeply fissured rocks that are more commonly seen in Yorkshire!

    Keep on the ridge, following occasional cairns and keeping Puig Mayor with its distinctive radar domes straight ahead. There is a 1049m spot height a little to the left – capture it if you wish.

    Another distinctive landmark is the triangular peak of L'Ofre.

    Pass a deep limestone chasm (note – there may be several of these, so take care) and keep below the peak on your left. Cross a wall at a rusting "private hunting" sign – a square divided diagonally into black and white – at **6hrs 15mins**.

13. Head towards a minor peak, following occasional cairns and keeping 20-30 metres away from the cliff on the left. Eventually (**6hrs 35mins**) you reach the end of the ridge. Curve round to the left of the final peak, and follow occasional cairns in the general direction of the refuge half-way up the hill ahead of you.

14. Dropping down the side of the peak, head slightly right and towards the trees at the top of the pass. Follow the clearly cairned pass, walk between the trees and across towards a concrete sign before the refuge, marking your route as being right to Sóller (**7hrs**) or straight on to the Mirador.

    Unless you're super-fit, or have plenty of time, take the Sóller turn at this point!

15. Follow the good, stony track which zigzags down to the Cornadors Pass. Pause to admire the L'Ofre farmhouse away to the right, then continue along the clear path through some trees. Eventually (**7hrs 15mins**) cross a bridge over a stream and you come to the wide cobbled track that goes all the way down the famous ravine called 'Es Barranc de Sóller'. Turn left along the stone-surfaced track and, after 5 minutes, pass through a gate.

16. Go down the track – seemingly endlessly. At **7hrs 45mins**, pass a couple of summer dwellings, the latter with an allotment.

A long way from Sóller to do some gardening!

Continue downhill, crossing four bridges and eventually approach the hamlet of Biniaraix.

17. Arrive in the small village square **(8hrs 45mins)** at the end of a long day.

June Parker, author of Walking in Mallorca (Cicerone Press) had few kind words to say about the Alfàbia ridge, but we will all agree with her that by finishing the walk in Biniaraix, you have the incentive of freshly squeezed orange juice. Rest your weary feet and enjoy one of the best cold drinks of your life.

Relaxed and refreshed, continue downhill, down the stepped street, along a tarmac lane and across a bridge. Then, head towards the ornate crosses below Biniaraix. From here, head straight towards Sóller town centre, eventually along the famous Carrer de la Lluna (see Walk 18) and back to Plaça de sa Constitució after at least 9 hours of wonderful walking.

Congratulations: this has been a day to remember. Also reflect on the fact that few people have completed this mountain adventure. Some may think it foolhardy, I say that life is about challenge and risk. When my friend Brian and I returned in pitch darkness from this walk, we decided that we were amongst the fortunate few.

Other walks and places of interest

If you have completed this walk, you are perfectly capable of grabbing a map and compass and planning your own walks. I have to confess to a degree of favouritism as I have a soft spot for Sóller and the many beautiful walks around the wonderful old town. Do try out the other walks in this section and tell me about your experiences. Write to:

Graham Beech, c/o Sigma Press, Stobart House, Pontyclerc, Penybanc Road, Ammanford, Carmarthenshire SA18 3HP

If you have walks in Mallorca that you'd like to share with others, please visit my website: www.bestmallorcawalks.co.uk